OPPOSING VIEWPOINTS® SERIES

Election Spending

W9-AQN-126

Other Books of Related Interest:

Opposing Viewpoints Series

The Banking Crisis

Church and State

The Federal Budget

Judicial Activism

Presidential Powers

At Issue Series

Campaign Finance

The Federal Budget Deficit

How Does Religion Influence Politics?

Voter Fraud

Current Controversies Series

Capitalism

Federal Elections

The Tea Party Movement

The US Economy

US Government Corruption

"Congress shall make no law . . . abridging the freedom of speech, or of the press."

First Amendment to the US Constitution

The basic foundation of our democracy is the First Amendment guarantee of freedom of expression. The Opposing Viewpoints series is dedicated to the concept of this basic freedom and the idea that it is more important to practice it than to enshrine it.

**OPPOSING
VIEWPOINTS®
SERIES**

Election Spending

Nancy Dziedzic, Book Editor

GREENHAVEN PRESS
A part of Gale, Cengage Learning

I.C.C. LIBRARY

**GALE
CENGAGE Learning**

Detroit • New York • San Francisco • New Haven, Conn • Waterville, Maine • London

Elizabeth Des Chenes, *Managing Editor*

© 2012 Greenhaven Press, a part of Gale, Cengage Learning

Gale and Greenhaven Press are registered trademarks used herein under license.

For more information, contact:
Greenhaven Press
27500 Drake Rd.
Farmington Hills, MI 48331-3535
Or you can visit our Internet site at gale.cengage.com

LIBRARY OF CONGRESS CATALOGING-IN-PUBLICATION DATA

Election spending / Nancy Dziedzic, book editor.
 p. cm. -- (Opposing viewpoints)
 Includes bibliographical references and index.
 ISBN 978-0-7377-5434-6 (hardcover) -- ISBN 978-0-7377-5435-3 (pbk.)
 1. Campaign funds--United States. I. Dziedzic, Nancy G.
 JK1991.E543 2011
 324.7'80973--dc22
                                                   2011014481

Printed in the United States of America
1 2 3 4 5 6 7 15 14 13 12 11

Contents

Chapter 3: Does Campaign Finance Reform Effectively Regulate Election Spending?

Chapter 4: How Does the *Citizens United* Decision Affect Constitutional Rights?

Why Consider Opposing Viewpoints?

> "The only way in which a human being can make some approach to knowing the whole of a subject is by hearing what can be said about it by persons of every variety of opinion and studying all modes in which it can be looked at by every character of mind. No wise man ever acquired his wisdom in any mode but this."
>
> *John Stuart Mill*

In our media-intensive culture it is not difficult to find differing opinions. Thousands of newspapers and magazines and dozens of radio and television talk shows resound with differing points of view. The difficulty lies in deciding which opinion to agree with and which "experts" seem the most credible. The more inundated we become with differing opinions and claims, the more essential it is to hone critical reading and thinking skills to evaluate these ideas. Opposing Viewpoints books address this problem directly by presenting stimulating debates that can be used to enhance and teach these skills. The varied opinions contained in each book examine many different aspects of a single issue. While examining these conveniently edited opposing views, readers can develop critical thinking skills such as the ability to compare and contrast authors' credibility, facts, argumentation styles, use of persuasive techniques, and other stylistic tools. In short, the Opposing Viewpoints Series is an ideal way to attain the higher-level thinking and reading skills so essential in a culture of diverse and contradictory opinions.

In addition to providing a tool for critical thinking, Opposing Viewpoints books challenge readers to question their own strongly held opinions and assumptions. Most people form their opinions on the basis of upbringing, peer pressure, and personal, cultural, or professional bias. By reading carefully balanced opposing views, readers must directly confront new ideas as well as the opinions of those with whom they disagree. This is not to argue simplistically that everyone who reads opposing views will—or should—change his or her opinion. Instead, the series enhances readers' understanding of their own views by encouraging confrontation with opposing ideas. Careful examination of others' views can lead to the readers' understanding of the logical inconsistencies in their own opinions, perspective on why they hold an opinion, and the consideration of the possibility that their opinion requires further evaluation.

Evaluating Other Opinions

To ensure that this type of examination occurs, Opposing Viewpoints books present all types of opinions. Prominent spokespeople on different sides of each issue as well as well-known professionals from many disciplines challenge the reader. An additional goal of the series is to provide a forum for other, less known, or even unpopular viewpoints. The opinion of an ordinary person who has had to make the decision to cut off life support from a terminally ill relative, for example, may be just as valuable and provide just as much insight as a medical ethicist's professional opinion. The editors have two additional purposes in including these less known views. One, the editors encourage readers to respect others' opinions—even when not enhanced by professional credibility. It is only by reading or listening to and objectively evaluating others' ideas that one can determine whether they are worthy of consideration. Two, the inclusion of such viewpoints encourages the important critical thinking skill of objectively evaluating an author's credentials and bias. This evaluation will illuminate an author's reasons for taking a particular stance on an issue and will aid in readers' evaluation of the author's ideas.

It is our hope that these books will give readers a deeper understanding of the issues debated and an appreciation of the complexity of even seemingly simple issues when good and honest people disagree. This awareness is particularly important in a democratic society such as ours in which people enter into public debate to determine the common good. Those with whom one disagrees should not be regarded as enemies but rather as people whose views deserve careful examination and may shed light on one's own.

Thomas Jefferson once said that "difference of opinion leads to inquiry, and inquiry to truth." Jefferson, a broadly educated man, argued that "if a nation expects to be ignorant and free . . . it expects what never was and never will be." As individuals and as a nation, it is imperative that we consider the opinions of others and examine them with skill and discernment. The Opposing Viewpoints series is intended to help readers achieve this goal.

David L. Bender and Bruno Leone,
Founders

Introduction

> "I see in the near future a crisis approaching that unnerves me and causes me to tremble for the safety of my country. . . . Corporations have been enthroned and an era of corruption in high places will follow, and the money power of the country will endeavor to prolong its reign by working on the prejudices of the people until all wealth is aggregated in a few hands, and the Republic is destroyed."
>
> —Abraham Lincoln, 1864

Prior to the 2004 presidential election, few Americans had heard of 527 organizations. But when Democratic nominee Senator John Kerry ran against incumbent Republican George W. Bush, a controversy exploded over the way certain groups—the 527s—appeared to fund and endorse their candidate of choice. Ultimately, one of those 527s would do enough damage to Kerry's reputation in the public's eyes to affect the outcome of the election and raise questions about the senator's record in the Navy despite his years of distinguished service during the Vietnam War.

After 2002, 527 organizations emerged, when the Bipartisan Campaign Reform Act (BCRA; also known as the McCain-Feingold Act, after its sponsors, Arizona Senator John McCain and Wisconsin Senator Russ Feingold) banned "soft money" contributions to political parties. Soft money came from contributions that could not be used to campaign for specific candidates but could be used for "party-building" activities, such as funding television advertisements that showed images of a candidate and then simply encouraged viewers to support that candidate's party. Often, though, soft money was collected and secretly given to candidates' campaigns because it was not regulated by the 1971 Federal Election Campaign Act. In 1976, the Supreme Court heard the case *Buckley v. Valeo* and decided in favor of limits on the amount of money contributors could donate to campaigns but against putting a cap on the amount candidates could spend on their campaigns. Parties and their candidates realized that the unregulated soft money could be shifted around without attracting much notice, and, alongside the high court's pronouncement that a federal campaign spending limit would interfere with candidates' First Amendment rights, campaign spending took off, frequently with the unsavory result of introducing corruption and secrecy into a system intended to support freedom of speech.

After the passage of the BCRA, however, and with unregulated money off the table, 527s rose to take the place of soft money contributions. Named after the section of the US Tax Code under which they fall, 527 organizations were intended to provide political advocacy groups with a way to maintain their status as nonprofit organizations while allowing them to engage in political activities, which nonprofit groups that fall under other sections of the tax code are prohibited from doing. Again, a system was created that defied the intentions of its creators. What was supposed to benefit small donors, encourage political participation, and inspire free speech instead favored large-scale contributions from secretive donors who preferred to buy advertising space rather than openly debate opponents. The "shadow group" in political campaigning was born.

John Kerry first ran for Senate in 1984. A decorated veteran of the Vietnam War, he had been awarded three Purple Hearts, a Silver Star, and a Bronze Star for leadership and courage during his service. But upon his return from active duty in 1970, Kerry, like many other Vietnam veterans, had a change of heart and joined the group Vietnam Veterans Against the War (VVAW). Kerry testified before Congress in April 1971 on what he considered the injustices of the way the war was being executed and was considered to be a formidable opponent by President Richard Nixon's administration. When Kerry ran for president in 2004, his war record was well established in the military despite his subsequent disillusionment, and he had served as the Democratic senator from Massachusetts since January 1985.

So it was surprising when a 527 group called Swift Boat Veterans for Truth aired a series of television ads in three swing states (beginning in August 2004) featuring a group of former Vietnam War veterans claiming to have served with Kerry and maintaining that he had lied about his wartime record, had betrayed his fellow veterans, and was unfit to serve as president. Media outlets quickly seized on the fact that only one of the members of the group of 250 had actually served with Kerry, and none had apparently been in the same places at the same time. As reporters continued to investigate, the stories of the Swift Boat Veterans gradually fell apart and, more damning, connections to the Republican Party and to George W. Bush in particular were revealed despite the group's claim to be a nonpartisan group of veterans who were simply interested in setting the record straight for the good of their country. Nevertheless, the four ads put out by the Swift Boat Veterans—which, it turned out, had been 50 percent funded by just three individuals, all millionaire Texas businessmen with ties to the Bush campaign—left an indelible impression on American voters. Although the Swift Boat Veterans' stories were either proven false or were unverifiable, the well-financed group had managed to damage Kerry's reputation and, in the meantime, had secured for themselves a permanent place in history: The term "swift boating" has come to refer to any political character attack or smear campaign.

Although the Swift Boat Veterans for Truth was fined by the Federal Election Commission (FEC) in 2006, and the liberal-leaning Moveon.org Voter Fund also was fined for violating the terms of its 527 status during the 2004 election (and the group disbanded in 2008), 527 groups have flourished as sources of money in federal elections, especially in the wake of the groundbreaking January 2010 *Citizens United v. Federal Election Commission* campaign spending case decision by the Supreme Court. According to *Miller-McCune*'s Emily Badger, on January 19, 2011, $294.2 million was spent on the 2010 federal midterm elections—compared with $301.7 million on the 2008 presidential election. "Groups that didn't disclose to the FEC any information about the sources of their money," Badger writes, "spent a combined $135.6 million (or 46 percent of the total)." Furthermore, "Nearly half of the total, $138.5 million, came from just 10 groups. And seven of those organizations—including the ambiguously named American Action Network, American Future Fund, and Americans for Job Security—provided no donor information." All of those groups were 527s.

Robert Weissman, president of the watchdog organization Public Citizen, wrote in a January 2011 editorial for *McClatchy*: "Most of the outside money was funneled through a small number of groups, led by the US Chamber of Commerce and two [Republican political analyst] Karl Rove-affiliated operations. Most of the groups were funded by a small number of corporations and superwealthy individuals. And their spending had a disproportionate influence on the election."

This book explores major issues in the debate over election spending. Chapter 1, "Is Election Spending Influenced by Campaign Donor Disclosure?" examines the pros and cons of legislation that would mandate disclosure of the identities of campaign donors. In Chapter 2, "How Would Publicly Funded Elections Change the Campaign Process?" viewpoint authors debate whether or not elections should be financed using taxpayer money. Chapter 3, "Does Campaign Finance Reform Effectively Regulate Election Spending?" discusses whether reform efforts can bring about change. And Chapter 4, "How Does the *Citizens United* Decision Affect Constitutional Rights?" examines the issues surrounding the Supreme Court's decision in the *Citizens United* case. The viewpoints explored in *Opposing Viewpoints: Election Spending* will help readers understand the ongoing debate about this controversial aspect of democracy in America.

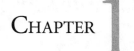

CHAPTER 1

Is Election Spending Influenced by Campaign Donor Disclosure?

Chapter Preface

The issue of campaign donor disclosure has proponents of two radically differing positions. Supporters of full disclosure maintain that democracy can be served—and corruption eliminated—only if the identities of all donors to election campaigns are made public. As it stands, political campaigns at the federal level must provide to the Federal Election Commission (FEC) the names, addresses, employer names, and telephone numbers of everyone who donates more than $200 in an election cycle, and campaigns must disclose information about those contributing $1,000 or more toward the production of an "electioneering communication"—an advertisement for television, radio, or satellite broadcast that refers to a federal candidate and is aired within thirty days of a primary vote or within sixty days of a general election. And even in its highly controversial *Citizens United v. Federal Election Commission* decision, the US Supreme Court agreed that strong disclosure legislation would mitigate any potentially corruptive influence from large corporate donations. Justice Anthony Kennedy wrote in the decision: "The First Amendment protects political speech; and disclosure permits citizens and shareholders to react to the speech of corporate entities in a proper way. This transparency enables the electorate to make informed decisions and give proper weight to different speakers and messages."

But another school of thought advances a completely different view of the need for transparency in campaign donations. Although public opinion polls indicate that nearly half of American voters object to anonymous political donations, some commentators advocate a system of complete anonymity wherein all political donations would be filtered through a type of clearinghouse and then doled out to the party or campaign intended by their donors. Supporters of this type of system contend that, because politicians would have no way of knowing the source of contributions, they would not feel beholden to any particular donors, and the possibility of corruption would be eliminated. These advocates frequently refer to the early American tradition of anonymous political speech, noting that the writers of the famed *Federalist Papers*—the collection of eighty-five essays by Alexander Hamilton, John Jay, and James Madison published in 1787 and 1788 arguing in favor of the ratification of the US Constitution—chose to publish their work under the collective pseudonym "Publius" so they could express themselves freely without fear of retribution. Such advocates also point out that anonymous political speech has in the past been a civil rights issue, ensuring that opponents of social reform could not retaliate with violence if they did not know who was supporting pro-civil rights legislation and candidates. Bradley Smith, a former chairman of the Federal Election Commission, has cited Supreme Court cases that demonstrated the need for nondisclosure: "The most prominent one is probably *NAACP [National Association for the Advancement of Colored People] v. Alabama* (1964), when Alabama wanted to know who was funding the NAACP's activities. We can see how that would be intimidating. Then there's *McIntyre v. Ohio Elections Commission* (1995). [Margaret] McIntyre was doing anonymous brochures against a school tax, which all the school officials supported. She had children in the schools who needed grades and access to such things as athletic teams and bands. She didn't necessarily want her name known, even though it was important for her to fight this issue."

The viewpoints in the following chapter discuss the issue of disclosure and how it relates to campaign spending, privacy rights, and the First Amendment right to free speech.

> "Under current disclosure laws for fed-
> eral elections, it's virtually impossible
> for the public to track how much a
> business spends, what it's spending on,
> or who ultimately benefits."

Lack of Disclosure Corrupts the Political System

Chisun Lee

Chisun Lee is an attorney, journalist, and staff writer for Pro-
Publica. In the following viewpoint, Lee argues that business
groups hope to strike down existing disclosure laws and prevent
new ones from being passed in order to further conceal their do-
nors. Although current disclosure laws provide for some trans-
parency in corporate campaign donations, Lee maintains, for the
most part they still prevent the public from obtaining informa-
tion about who donates, how much is donated, and what the
aim of the donation is. When companies donate to a nonprofit
trade group such as the US Chamber of Commerce, Lee points
out, the group's donation records are kept confidential. Whereas
when companies contribute directly to a campaign or buy adver-
tising time on their own, they are subject to disclosure laws. And

Chisun Lee, "Higher Corporate Spending on Election Ads Could Be All but Invisible,"
ProPublica, March 10, 2010. Copyright © 2010 by ProPublica.com. Reproduced by permission.

while thirty-nine states require some degree of disclosure in political advertising, Lee asserts, only five lack the loopholes that allow corporations to skirt the laws altogether.

As you read, consider the following questions:

1. For what reason would a company choose not to spend money in politics, according to Lee?

2. According to the author, how much did the US Chamber of Commerce spend on advertising, lobbying, and activism in 2009?

3. How many states have laws that mandate some level of disclosure?

The Supreme Court recently freed corporations to spend more money on aggressive election ads [in the January 2010 *Citizens United v. Federal Election Commission* ruling]. But if businesses take advantage of this new freedom, the public probably won't know it, because it's easy for them to legally hide their political spending.

Under current disclosure laws for federal elections, it's virtually impossible for the public to track how much a business spends, what it's spending on, or who ultimately benefits. Experts say the transparency problem extends to state and local races as well.

"There is no good way to gauge" how much any given company spends on elections, said Karl Sandstrom, a former vice chairman of the Federal Election Commission [FEC] and counsel to the Center for Political Accountability. "There's no central collection of the information, no monitoring."

Fears of Consumer and Shareholder Backlash

Companies invest in politics to win favorable regulations or block those "that could choke off their business model," said Robert Kelner, chairman of Covington & Burling's Washington, D.C., political law group. But they'd rather hide these political activities, he said, because they fear backlash from customers or shareholders.

For instance, a company may want to help Democratic politicians who support health care reforms that would benefit the company, but it worries about offending "Republican shareholders who may care more about their personal ideology than about their three shares of stock in the company," said Kelner, who says he represents many politically active Fortune 500 companies. "The same would be true on the other side of the political spectrum."

Businesses must reveal their identities on public reports to the Federal Election Commission if they buy advertising on their own. But one popular and perfectly legal conduit for companies wanting to influence politics under the radar is to give money to nonprofit trade groups such as the U.S. Chamber of Commerce.

The US Chamber of Commerce Conceals Donors

The Chamber and its national affiliates spent $144.5 million last year [2009] on advertising, lobbying and grass-roots activism—more than either the Republican or Democratic party spent, according to a Center for Responsive Politics analysis of public records—while legally concealing the names of its funders. *The Los Angeles Times* reported this week [March 2010] that the Chamber is building a grass-roots political operation that has signed up about 6 million non-Chamber members.

Some of the positions the Chamber has successfully advanced on behalf of its donors include a nationwide campaign to unseat state judges who were considered tough on corporate defendants and opposition to a federal bill that would have criminalized defective auto manufacturing.

Now the Jan. 21 [2010] Supreme Court ruling that increases the potential political clout of businesses is drawing fresh attention to the problem of tracking them.

Citizens United and Corporate Ads

That decision, *Citizens United v. Federal Election Commission*, allows corporations to run television ads that don't merely speak to an issue but say outright whether a candidate should be elected, and allows them to do so any time they want to, using their general funds. The ruling also gives nonprofit groups like the Chamber these new freedoms, because they are technically structured as corporations.

Before, corporations had to rely on employee and shareholder contributions to a separate political account to finance the most explicit commercials and, in the months before an election, any issue ads that mentioned a candidate. Although the decision addressed federal election rules, its constitutional rationale also dismantles similar restrictions in 24 states.

Soon after the ruling, two Democrats—Rep. Chris Van Hollen of Maryland and Sen. Charles E. Schumer of New York—announced they were writing a bill to make it easier to tell which companies are backing which ads in federal elections. An outline of that bill, which is expected to be introduced this week [March 2010], proposes forcing nonprofit groups to identify those who fund their political commercials.

At present, nonprofit groups don't have to disclose the sources of their advertising money, unless the donors specified that their contributions were intended for political ads.

"Unless you're sort of dumb enough to designate your contribution to the Chamber," said Meredith McGehee, policy director of the Campaign Legal Center, "no one will ever know who's the source of those funds."

Business Groups Have More Funds

Politically active nonprofits exist across the ideological and policy spectrum and include unions as well as trade groups.

Their funders include both corporations and individuals, some of them very wealthy. But campaign finance experts say groups that advocate specifically for business tend to have the greatest resources, simply because corporations have the most money to give.

The lack of tracking mechanisms sometimes leaves company officials themselves in the dark about their organization's political activities, said Adam Kanzer, managing director and general counsel of Domini Social Investments, which files shareholder resolutions to push corporations to adopt self-monitoring and disclosure practices.

"In a lot of our conversations with companies, they say, 'We don't know exactly how our money is getting spent. It's hard to get those answers,'" Kanzer said. One major drug manufacturer, he said, signed on for voluntary disclosure after learning that its funds had supported a state judicial campaign that many voters—who could be customers or shareholders—viewed as racist.

The public price of spotty disclosure is not being able to gauge the real effects of corporation-backed politics, McGehee said. She questioned one argument, often made by defenders of the *Citizens United* decision, that the 26 states that have long allowed unlimited corporate advertising in their elections haven't suffered more political corruption than the rest of the nation.

"How would you know? Most of those states have next to no disclosure," McGehee said. Corporations "could be buying outcomes left and right, but because of no disclosure, we don't know." A 2007 examination by the National Institute on Money in State Politics found that, while 39 states required some degree of disclosure by political advertisers, the laws in most were riddled with loopholes. Only five states required enough detail to link sponsors with specific ads, the report said.

The *Citizens United* Ruling Is a Threat to Financial Stability

Citizens United [v. Federal Election Commission ruling by the Supreme Court] imperils not only our democracy. It also threatens the U.S. economy. *Citizens United* adds to the existing institutional tools that encourage a "corruption economy," long known to waste social resources and reward inefficiency. This economy also systematically disadvantages startups and "disruptive innovators"—companies and individuals whose ideas productively displace entrenched alternatives. . . .

In a corruption economy, established companies are given the upper hand. They have legions of lobbyists, revenue to allocate to campaign expenditures, and deep and long relationships with legislators. Upstarts usually have none of that, so established companies use their greater access to government and legal avenues to kill off young competitors. For instance, when a new data format (from home video to YouTube) hits the market, established content providers often file copyright complaints. Following similar logic, established telecom companies attempt to interfere with Internet traffic. This changes the behavior of new companies for the worse. An upstart's first idea should be a product or service, not an appropriations rider; its first employees should be engineers, investors, and management, not lobbyists and lawyers.

Marvin Ammori,
"Corruption Economy," Boston Review,
September–October 2010.

Legislation Would Track the Money

Rep. Van Hollen said the disclosure requirements he and Schumer are drafting would uncover the corporate political money flowing through nonprofit channels.

"If corporations spend money in these campaigns, we cannot allow them to hide behind sham organizations and dummy corporations that mislead voters," he said in a written comment to *ProPublica*. "Voters have a right to know who is delivering and paying for the message."

The requirements would apply to unions and liberal nonprofits as well as trade groups, according to the early outline of the bill. The proposal mentions additional transparency requirements—such as mandating corporate disclosures to shareholders and "stand by your ad" appearances by CEOs [chief executive officers] of companies that finance commercials directly—and seeks outright bans on political advertising by government contractors, bailout recipients and companies significantly controlled by foreigners.

A strong disclosure law would be "hugely effective" in revealing who is paying for political speech, said Trevor Potter, a former FEC chairman and head lawyer for [Senator] John McCain's presidential campaigns, who is now general counsel at Campaign Legal Center.

But precisely for that reason, Potter said, politics may get in the way of any serious reform. He expects trade groups on the right, unions on the left and other cause groups across the board to fight hard against such legislation.

Already the political battle is taking shape.

Partisan Disagreement About Legislation

Asked to comment on the push for more disclosure, the Chamber's chief legal officer and general counsel, Steven Law, instead attacked the political motives of the proponents. "Unions overwhelmingly support those who are pushing this legislation," he said in an e-mail. "This isn't about reform, it's about politicians trying to secure advantages for themselves before an election."

That reaction drew fire from one of the nation's most politically active unions, the Service Employees International Union [SEIU], which also declined to comment on the new disclosure proposals. "The coming flood of corporate and foreign money into our elections through the U.S. Chamber of Commerce is a threat to democracy, plain and simple," said Anna Burger, SEIU's secretary-treasurer, in an e-mail. She called on legislators to "drag the Chamber's practices into the light of day."

The Chamber revealed more about its view of disclosure in an amicus brief it filed in the *Citizens United* case on behalf of the 3 million business members it says it has. It supported the plaintiff, a nonprofit corporation called Citizens United, which wanted the Supreme Court not only to lift corporate advertising bans but also to strike down the existing disclosure requirements.

The Chamber argued that those requirements inhibited corporations from speaking out. If the public discovered that corporations were "taking controversial positions," it might punish them, the brief said. As an example, it pointed to a 2005 boycott of ExxonMobil products after the public learned the company was lobbying Congress to open the Arctic National Wildlife Refuge to drilling.

That argument failed to persuade the high court, which by an 8-1 majority decided to leave the current disclosure laws intact.

Transparency is important, wrote Justice Anthony Kennedy for the majority, because it helps voters "give proper weight to different speakers and messages," and because it allows citizens to "see whether elected officials are 'in the pocket' of so-called moneyed interests."

> "Disclosure has resulted in government-
> enabled invasions of privacy—and
> sometimes outright harassment—and
> it has added to a political climate in
> which candidates are judged by their
> funders rather than their ideas."

Disclosure Laws Are an Invasion of Privacy

Bradley A. Smith

Bradley A. Smith is a professor of law at Capital University Law School in Columbus, Ohio, chairman of the Center for Competitive Politics, and a former chairman of the Federal Election Commission. In the following viewpoint, Smith likens anonymous political donations to the secret ballot, arguing that forcing voters—particularly small donors—to disclose their political donations amounts to an invasion of privacy. Imagining a Patriot Act II, in which the government would collect the personal information of all donors to political campaigns and nonprofit groups to keep terrorists from influencing American elections, Smith declares that this violation of civil rights already exists, in the form of political disclosure legislation. Because the public does not have the right to know the personal details of a person's life,

Bradley A. Smith, "In Defense of Political Anonymity," *City Journal*, Winter 2010. Copyright © 2010 by Manhattan Institute for Policy Research. Reproduced by permission.

writes Smith, neither should they have the right to know about a person's political donations, particularly because such information could be used for nefarious purposes.

As you read, consider the following questions:

1. What is the name of the 1972 law that first required disclosure of the personal information of certain political campaign donors?

2. What was the "K Street Project," according to Smith?

3. Which Founding Fathers wrote the *Federalist Papers*, and what was the pseudonym they used to publish anonymously?

I magine if the George W. Bush administration, in its waning days, had introduced something called the Patriot II Act. To prevent terrorists and foreign agents from influencing American governments and political parties, the act would require political campaigns and other groups to report the names, addresses, and employers of their supporters to the federal government, which would enter the information into a database. The act would also give businesses access to this database, enabling them to make hiring decisions, credit determinations, and other choices based on political activity. Can anyone doubt that Patriot II would be widely considered a gross violation of civil liberties?

Fortunately, the government never passed such a bill. Unfortunately, it didn't need to: this is already the law, and it has been for over 30 years. It is, in fact, one of the most popular laws in America: the Federal Election Campaign Act, which does indeed require campaigns, political parties, and certain citizens' groups engaged in politics to report the names, addresses, and employment information of their financial supporters. This information is maintained in a government database that is available to anyone—businesses, union bosses, local officials, nosy neighbors, and whoever else might be curious about somebody's politics.

The idea of *limiting* financial support of politics remains deeply controversial, even seven years after the passage of the so-called McCain-Feingold bill, [the Bipartisan Campaign Reform Act of 2002] which extended many of the Federal Election Campaign Act's limitations on contributions to previously unregulated political activities. Yet even the most ardent opponents of McCain-Feingold seldom question the disclosure requirements of the original 1972 act. So widely accepted is the idea that campaign contributions and personal information about donors ought to be public that many people don't even consider it regulation. When the First Amendment counsel for the ACLU [American Civil Liberties Union], the late Marv Johnson, met in 2006 with a prominent congressional reformer to argue against a proposal to regulate grassroots political activity, he was assured that no new "regulation" was contemplated—"just disclosure."

But it's far from clear that the forced disclosure of political contributions has benefited society. Disclosure has resulted in government-enabled invasions of privacy—and sometimes outright harassment—and it has added to a political climate in which candidates are judged by their funders rather than their ideas. . . .

Compulsory Disclosure Has Few Benefits

The idea that you should be compelled to reveal your political activity to the government is often justified by "the public's right to know." But the public doesn't, of course, have a right to know about most things that you do—about your job-performance reviews, income-tax returns, credit history, birth-control purchases, school grades, employment history, book purchases, dieting habits, or voting choices, to give just a few examples. Some of this information may become available to the public, but only because you volunteer it, not because the government mandates it. Why should your donations be any different?

One oft-heard answer is that the public has a right to be informed of influences, including financial influences, that might affect the judgment and actions of its elected representatives. It happens that the degree to which campaign contributions actually influence legislative behavior is hotly disputed in the professional literature. But set that aside for now and assume, as most casual observers and the Supreme Court do, that the possibility is there. Federal and state laws would still set the threshold for disclosure far too low. People who donate $20 to a Michigan candidate, or even $200 to a federal one, will exercise zero influence on the candidate if he's elected. That their contributions—and addresses and employers— need to be publicly disclosed to prevent corruption is a proposition that can scarcely be stated with a straight face.

Even where it arguably offers public benefits—as in the case of truly large individual contributions or institutional contributions from political action committees, corporations, or unions—compulsory disclosure brings with it rarely appreciated costs. Above all, it invites government officials to abuse their power. From 1995 through 2006, when Republicans controlled Congress, they executed the "K Street Project," using compulsory-disclosure data to compile a list of the 400 largest political action committees and their giving patterns. Affiliated lobbyists were then called into the offices of Republican leaders and shown their place in either a "friendly" or an "unfriendly" column. Democrats complained endlessly about the project, but when they regained the majority in 2007, they took advantage of compulsory disclosure and employed the same tactic. As one understandably anonymous lobbyist told the *Wall Street Journal* in 2007, Democrats quickly put out the word that "if you have an issue on trade, taxes, or regulation, you'd better be a donor and you'd better not be part of any effort to run ads against our freshmen incumbents." Disclosure is what makes the threats work. . . .

Disclosure Laws Face Numerous Challenges

James Bopp, the attorney who initiated *Citizens United [v. Federal Election Commission]* and a longtime member of the RNC [Republican National Committee] . . . has made no secret of the fact that his ultimate goal is the elimination of virtually *all* campaign finance restrictions including the reporting of donors. In January [2010], he told the *New York Times* that, "[g]roups have to be relieved of reporting their donors if lifting the prohibition on their political speech is going to have any meaning."

One disclosure case brought by Mr. Bopp—*Doe v. Reed*—was argued before the Supreme Court on April 28, 2010. *Doe v. Reed* does not address contributors, but rather the disclosure of referenda petition signatories in connection to a Washington state ballot referendum regarding domestic partnerships. But there are numerous cases that do seek to overturn contributor disclosure provisions in the lower courts. One such challenge was brought by Mr. Bopp on behalf of the inaptly named "Committee for Truth in Politics." This group is simultaneously suing the FEC [Federal Election Commission] to avoid disclosing its donors while spending millions of dollars airing factually unsupported attack ads against vulnerable candidates, for instance, calling the financial reform bill a "$4 trillion bailout for banks."

J. Gerald Hebert and Tara Malloy,
"Challenges to Campaign Finance and Disclosures Laws
Multiply after Citizens United *Ruling from Roberts Court,"*
Campaign Legal Center, May 21, 2010.

Sound Reasons for Anonymity

In the Republic's early days, it's important to remember, anonymous and pseudonymous political speech was common. The most famous example is The *Federalist Papers*, written by Alexander Hamilton, James Madison, and John Jay under the pseudonym "Publius." Countering their arguments for the proposed Constitution, prominent statesmen like Richard Henry Lee and Samuel Adams also wrote under pseudonyms, including "Federal Farmer," "Brutus," and "Candidus." Often, the newspapers in which these authors published their work were themselves supported by anonymous financiers. And in later years, many prominent Americans wrote anonymously, including Chief Justice John Marshall, who wrote as "a Friend of the Union" and "a Friend of the Constitution" to explain and elaborate his important opinion in *McCulloch v. Maryland*. Thomas Jefferson, Abraham Lincoln, and Winfield Scott anonymously subsidized political tracts and newspapers.

The great historian of The *Federalist Papers*, Clinton Rossiter, noted that the authors wrote pseudonymously for "sound political purposes." For one thing, they didn't want their disagreements to interfere with their other activities—a reason that remains valid today. For several years, Case Western law professor Jonathan Adler blogged pseudonymously as "Juan Non-Volokh" at the popular blog Volokh Conspiracy. As an untenured professor, Adler worried that his frank writing on political issues might compromise acceptance of his academic work. Former [George W.] Bush speechwriter David Frum explains why several contributors to his new website, Frum Forum, prefer to use pseudonyms: "Often, the contributor is a government employee concerned about the consequences of speaking too frankly about the work of his bureaucracy. In one case, the author was writing about wrongdoing by someone he regularly encountered socially."

This argument for anonymity applies to financial supporters of campaigns as well. In 2007, John Kerry and congressional Democrats vetoed the nomination of Republican donor Sam Fox to be ambassador to Belgium—not because Fox was unqualified but because he had contributed to Swift Boat Veterans for Truth, a group Kerry felt had unfairly criticized him in his 2004 presidential race. As Senator Chris Dodd explained in support of Kerry, Fox's "unwillingness to . . . express regret for providing $50,000 to bankroll the organization convinced me that he would not be an acceptable candidate to represent the United States." The message was clear: support a group that legislators deem too vigorous in its criticism, and the legislators will retaliate.

Disclosure Promotes Personal Attacks

A second reason that the *Federalist* authors wrote pseudonymously, Rossiter pointed out, was that they wanted to have their arguments debated on the merits, rather than through personal attacks. But disclosure fosters exactly the opposite idea: that the identity of the speaker matters more than the force of his argument. For example, in the 1990s, as term limits stormed to success after success, they suffered their only state-level ballot defeat in Washington State, after voters learned that funders of the measure included the libertarian Koch brothers. As Brian Doherty recounts in *Radicals for Capitalism*, "suddenly the fight was not about the wisdom of term limits, but the probity of eliminating drug laws and Social Security." In fact, the Supreme Court stated in *Buckley v. Valeo* that disclosure laws would "allow voters to place each candidate in the political spectrum more precisely than is often possible solely on the basis of party labels and campaign speeches." This amounts to an endorsement of ad hominem argument, whose ability to debase political debate the Founders understood very well.

A political culture that focuses excessively on the "who" rather than the "what"—one that fosters the view that if we know who wrote an opinion, it is not necessary to read the opinion itself—is not healthy. Look at the comments section in almost any political blog, on the left or the right, and you'll see comments almost uniformly taking a quick turn into attacks on the identity and motivation of the writers. The decline in the quality of our civic discourse can't be dumped entirely at the foot of mandatory disclosure, of course. But laws that regard the identity of speakers as fundamental to the public's ability to judge arguments may well exacerbate a thoughtless, partisan, nasty brand of political debate.

For 35 years, mandatory disclosure of political contributions has been the most popular part of the campaign-finance "reform" agenda. Yet the idea that Americans should report their political activity to the government is, in many ways, the most un-American part of that agenda. Excessive disclosure invades privacy to little benefit and provides government—and others—the information they need to retaliate against people holding unpopular or inconvenient views. Moreover, compulsory disclosure sends the message that identity, not ideas, matter. Call the result "ad hominem democracy," an atmosphere in which serious, civil debate about issues seems ever harder to find.

> *"Real time disclosure is imperative to shine the light on contributions as they pour into Congress. . . . Similarly, real time disclosure would aid the need for increased competition and speech in our politics."*

Donation Disclosure Promotes Political Engagement and Enhances Public Debate

Paul Blumenthal

Paul Blumenthal is a researcher and head writer for the Sunlight Foundation. His work has been featured in the New York Review of Books, New York Times, *on PBS's* Frontline, *and on National Public Radio. In the following viewpoint, Blumenthal argues that online fundraising portals that allow disclosure of political donors in real time will increase political participation and increase competition in election contests. When South Carolina Representative Joe Wilson broke congressional protocol by heckling President Barack Obama during his 2010 State of the Union address, the race between him and his Democratic oppo-*

Paul Blumenthal, "What Can 'You Lie' Tell Us about Real-Time Disclosure?" Sunlight Foundation.org, September 11, 2009. Copyright © 2009 by Sunlight Foundation. Reproduced by permission.

nent, Rob Miller, heated up significantly when donors immediately began contributing to Miller's campaign, and the results of the stepped-up donations were reported via an online portal in real time. Blumenthal argues that this is an example of the power of donor transparency to increase public participation in the political process and, ultimately, to strengthen the democratic ideal.

As you read, consider the following questions:

1. According the Blumenthal, what is one benefit of making donations to political races?

2. What is one benefit of being able to view contributions to the campaigns of opposing candidates in real time disclosure, according to Blumenthal?

3. What is the name of the Supreme Court decision that upheld the mandated disclosure of campaign contributions?

Rob Miller, a Marine and congressional candidate in South Carolina's 2nd district, probably didn't expect to become an overnight star while he was watching the President give a speech to a joint session of Congress on health care reform [September 2009]. Then came Rep. Joe Wilson's rebel yell, "You lie!" Miller is Wilson's Democratic opponent in 2010 and lost a relatively close election to Wilson in 2008 (54%-46%). The money started pouring in almost immediately. Within a few hours, Miller raised over $100,000. Two days after Wilson's outburst, Miller has raked in over $750,000 (while writing he has crept to almost $800,000), likely making him one of the better funded Democrats running for a House seat in 2010.

Nearly all of this money is being raised through the site ActBlue (http://www.actblue.com/), a fundraising portal set up to allow individuals to raise money for Democratic candidates themselves. One of the best features of the site is its transparency. The site updates as new contributions come in, showing

The Danger of Secret Donations

The partisan dimension should not distract from the larger problem facing American democracy. Secret money is dangerous. Secret money corrupts. Secret money is antithetical to the transparency that democracy requires. And concentrated money, . . . buys more influence and access than small contributions.

E.J. Dionne,
"Voters Are in the Dark on Campaign Spending,"
Washington Post, *October 25, 2010.*

the total on the candidate's page—or on a fundraising group's page (like this group raising money for Miller (http://www.actblue.com/entity/fundraisers/19079)). All of this has been written before, but I wanted to highlight one feature of this transparency: real time disclosure.

Current campaign finance laws require only quarterly disclosures of campaign contributions. The unforseen money bomb for Rob Miller exposes a problem with the limited system of quarterly disclosures for candidates trying to increase enthusiasm for and attract small donor money to their campaigns. The transparent nature of ActBlue allows for the snowballing effect we've seen over the past few days. It's a lot more rewarding for small donors to contribute when they can see the group results of their actions. Many campaigns have used transparent fundraising mechanisms at times, the Howard Dean bat and the Ron Paul money bomb are two obvious and innovative examples. By the 2008 campaign this was a pretty standard tactic of presidential candidates; both Barack Obama and Hillary Clinton used this gimic many times in the Democratic primary.

Real-Time Disclosure Increases Political Participation

But why shouldn't this just be the norm? Campaign contributions are viewed by the law as a form of speech. If we see real time disclosure of campaign funding help increase individual desire to contribute, isn't this a boon for speech and democratic participation? Donating to a campaign is a step above voting, in terms of participation, and can lead to further political actions like volunteering or even getting involved in local politics. Campaigns could simply forward their contributions on to the Federal Election Commission (FEC) in a timely, maybe not immediate, manner and the FEC could report the contributions in real time. This could increase transparency, campaign enthusiasm and small donor power across the board.

Right now, in the Miller/Wilson example we are seeing how the transparency of real time contributions has helped one candidate over another. Since Wilson's comment, the media has focused on his opponents rapid fundraising as they can see the numbers pour in over ActBlue. It took two days for Wilson to release a number on the amount he had raised, $200,000, in the wake of his outburst. A system where real time contributions could be viewed side-by-side may have helped increase contributions to Wilson. Who doesn't like a little healthy competition?

This is certainly a different argument for disclosure than is usually made, which is that money plays an influencing role in politics and disclosure of contributions is required to allow the public and an enforcement body to hold candidates accountable. This is an important argument and is certainly another reason for real time disclosure of contributions, but as I've stated above disclosure can also play a role in invigorating political activity. Unfortunately, it is the influence argument as the backbone of campaign disclosure that begins to complicate real time disclosure.

Real-Time Disclosure Raises Practical Concerns

One requirement in campaign finance disclosure is the disclosure of names and employment, a key to gleaning the influence interests and powerful people have with our elected representatives. In *Buckley v. Valeo* . . . the Supreme Court upheld the disclosure of campaign contributions due to the need to avert possible problems of corruption and influence in elections and determined a minimum threshold for disclosure. It was determined by the court that contributions of a certain value were more likely to cause undue influence or potential corruption than smaller donations. These small donors would be spared disclosure to protect their anonymity as the size of their donation could not reasonably be seen to influence a candidate. Thus we have a system where small donations— those who contributed less than $250—do not need to be disclosed to the FEC with the attendant name, employment and other categories for each individual donor.

How would this work out in a system of real time disclosure? Should we do away with minimum disclosure threshold? There were numerous problems with small donors during the 2008 elections, fraudulent donations and more, that could lead to a reasonable need for small donor disclosure. But would this work counter to the benefits of real time disclosure (increased participation, competition and speech) by scaring off individual donors afraid of identifying themselves? I'm not sure what the answer is to that question.

From the classic perspective of influence in politics, real time disclosure is imperative to shine the light on contributions as they pour into Congress during bill markups, committee hearings and votes. Similarly, real time disclosure would aid the need for increased competition and speech in our politics. Thanks to Rob Miller and Joe Wilson and ActBlue for showing us that.

> *"As anyone who has had their political yard signs torn down can imagine, with today's easy access to donor information on the Internet, any crank or unhinged individual can obtain information on his political opponents."*

Donor Disclosure Threatens the Privacy and Security of Small Contributors

John R. Lott Jr. and Bradley A. Smith

John R. Lott Jr. is a senior research scientist at the University of Maryland. Bradley A. Smith is a former commissioner of the Federal Election Commission, chairman of the Center for Competitive Politics, and professor of law at Capital University in Columbus, Ohio. In the following viewpoint, Lott and Smith find that mandated donor disclosure can have unwanted and sometimes dangerous consequences when individuals are punished with job termination, boycotts, or even violence because of their campaign contributions. According to Lott and Smith, much of the danger lies in disclosure legislation that includes not just election campaigns but also public referendums that seek to

John R. Lott Jr. and Bradley A. Smith, "Donor Disclosure Has Its Downsides," *Wall Street Journal* online, December 26, 2008. Copyright © 2008 by Wall Street Journal. Reproduced by permission of the authors.

adopt local and statewide proposals. The authors cite California's controversial Proposition 8, which sought to ban gay marriage in that state, as a case that put donors both in favor of and against the proposal in danger of job loss, economic peril, and even physical violence. Lott and Smith maintain that anonymity has served an important role in the American democratic process from the beginning.

As you read, consider the following questions:

1. What is Proposition 8?

2. According to the authors, what recourse do voters have on the donor disclosure issue?

3. Which Supreme Court ruling first addressed the First Amendment rights of supporters of nonprofit groups?

How would you like elections without secret ballots? To most people, this would be absurd.

We have secret balloting for obvious reasons. Politics frequently generates hot tempers. People can put up yard signs or wear political buttons if they want. But not everyone feels comfortable making his or her positions public—many worry that their choice might offend or anger someone else. They fear losing their jobs or facing boycotts of their businesses.

And yet the mandatory public disclosure of financial donations to political campaigns in almost every state and at the federal level renders people's fears and vulnerability all too real. Proposition 8—California's recently passed [November 2008] constitutional amendment to outlaw gay marriage by ensuring that marriage in that state remains between a man and a woman—is a dramatic case in point. Its passage has generated retaliation against those who supported it, once their financial support was made public and put online.

Donors Face Boycotts and Intimidation

For example, when it was discovered that Scott Eckern, director of the nonprofit California Musical Theater in Sacramento, had given $1,000 to Yes on 8, the theater was deluged with criticism from prominent artists. Mr. Eckern was forced to resign.

Richard Raddon, the director of the L.A. [Los Angeles] Film Festival, donated $1,500 to Yes on 8. A threatened boycott and picketing of the next festival forced him to resign. Alan Stock, the chief executive of the Cinemark theater chain, gave $9,999. Cinemark is facing a boycott, and so is the gay-friendly Sundance Film Festival because it uses a Cinemark theater to screen some of its films.

A Palo Alto dentist lost patients as a result of his $1,000 donation. A restaurant manager in Los Angeles gave a $100 personal donation, triggering a demonstration and boycott against her restaurant. The pressure was so intense that Marjorie Christoffersen, who had managed the place for 26 years, resigned.

These are just a few instances that have come to light, and the ramifications are still occurring over a month after the election. The larger point of this spectacle is its implications for the future: to intimidate people who donate to controversial campaigns.

Political Preferences Should Remain Private

The question is not whether Prop. 8 should have passed, but whether its supporters (or opponents) should have their political preferences protected in the same way that voters are protected. Is there any reason to think that the repercussions Mr. Eckern faced for donating to Prop. 8 would be different if it were revealed that instead of donating, he had voted for it?

Indeed, supporters of Prop. 8 engaged in pressure tactics. At least one businessman who donated to "No on 8," Jim Abbott of Abbott & Associates, a real estate firm in San Diego, received a letter from the Prop. 8 Executive Committee threatening to publish his company's name if he didn't also donate to the "Yes on 8" campaign.

In each case, the law required disclosure of these individuals' financial support for Prop. 8. Supposedly, the reason for requiring disclosure of campaign contributions is to allow voters to police politicians who might otherwise become beholden to financiers by letting voters know "who is behind the message." But in a referendum vote such as Prop. 8, there are no office holders to be beholden to big donors.

Does anyone believe that in campaigns costing millions of dollars a donation of $100, or even $1,000 or $10,000 will give the donor "undue" influence? Over whom? Meanwhile, voters learn little by knowing the names and personal information of thousands of small contributors.

Besides, it is not the case that voters would have no recourse when it comes to the financial backers of politicians or initiatives. Even without mandatory disclosure rules, the unwillingness to release donation information can itself become a campaign issue. If voters want to know who donated, there will be pressure to disclose that information. Possibly voters will be most concerned about who the donors are when regulatory issues are being debated. But that is for them to decide. They can always vote "no."

Anonymity Protects Donors

Ironically, it has long been minorities who have benefited the most from anonymous speech. In the 1950s, for example, Southern states sought to obtain membership lists of the NAACP [National Association for the Advancement of Colored People] in the name of the public's "right to know." Such disclosure would have destroyed the NAACP's financial base in the South and opened its supporters to threats and violence. It took a Supreme Court ruling in *NAACP v. Alabama* (1958) to protect the privacy of the NAACP and its supporters on First Amendment grounds. And more recently, it has usually been supporters of gay rights who have preferred to keep their support quiet.

There is another problem with publicizing donations in political elections: It tends to entrench powerful politicians whom donors fear alienating. If business executives give money to a committee chairman's opponent, they often fear retribution.

Other threats are more personal. For example, in 2004 Gigi Brienza contributed $500 to the John Edwards presidential campaign. An extremist animal rights group used that information to list Ms. Brienza's home address (and similarly, that of dozens of co-workers) on a Web site, under the ominous heading, "Now you know where to find them." Her "offense," also revealed from the campaign finance records, was that she worked for a pharmaceutical company that tested its products on animals.

In the aftermath of Prop. 8 we can glimpse a very ugly future. As anyone who has had their political yard signs torn down can imagine, with today's easy access to donor information on the Internet, any crank or unhinged individual can obtain information on his political opponents, including work and home addresses, all but instantaneously. When even donations as small as $100 trigger demonstrations, it is hard to know how one will feel safe in supporting causes one believes in.

"We need a federally chartered clearing-house for campaign donations that matches donors to designated, registered candidates and political action committees."

Fully Anonymous Campaign Donations Will Eliminate Political Corruption

Marc Geffroy and R.R. Reno

Marc Geffroy owns a business in Maryland. R.R. Reno is a professor at Creighton University in Omaha, Nebraska, and is an editor of the journal First Things, *published by the Institute on Religion and Public Life. In the following viewpoint, Geffroy and Reno support a system of anonymous political donations, arguing that donors would be able to express their political opinions with unlimited contributions and that candidates would be less inclined toward corruption because they would never know who had donated to their campaign. Acknowledging that the current system of campaign donations is corrupt, the authors advocate a federal clearinghouse that would collect and then distribute donations to registered candidates and political action committees, eliminating the chance that elected officials could be influenced by money. Additionally, say Geffroy and Reno, a system of anonymity would allow leaders to focus on policy issues and the free exchange of ideas rather than the problems inherent in campaigning.*

As you read, consider the following questions:

1. What kind of system of donor anonymity do the authors propose to counter the purchase of political influence?

2. In what ways would free speech be upheld with mandated donor anonymity, according to the authors?

3. What do the authors claim would be eliminated by anonymous donations?

Much has been made of the Supreme Court's ruling in *Citizens United v. Federal Election Commission*, which rightly overturned an untenable and unfair suppression of financial contributions for political causes. Unfortunately, the decision is akin to performing surgery on a dying patient.

Our system of campaign finance is corrupt. Money floods into campaign coffers, but rarely because of a heartfelt desire to advance a political cause. The three most important words in Washington are access, access, access. Money, of course, buys access.

There is a way to break the iron grip on access that campaign contributions provide. The United States should establish an anonymous campaign finance system. We need a federally chartered clearinghouse for campaign donations that matches donors to designated, registered candidates and political action committees. Under such a system, politicians would not know who supports their careers, er, causes.

Anonymous Donations Would Limit Corruption

It's a simple but powerful concept. The identity of the campaign donor would be kept secret, which would break the wink-and-nod link between money and the legislative process.

Imagine the confusion on Capitol Hill. Members of Congress wouldn't know exactly whom to reward with special carve-outs. Union leaders might say they're big supporters of certain candidates, but who could know for sure?

The benefits of an anonymous system would be significant. We would see tighter, more issue-focused campaigns with smaller budgets. Lobbyists would still have jobs, but their roles would be more focused on providing information and analysis rather than bundling campaign donations and hosting reelection receptions.

The obvious objection is that anonymity seems to run counter to the idea of free speech. If nobody knows you're contributing, your efforts to signal your support fail. But the First Amendment concerns the unfettered flow of ideas—not the free flow of money and influence.

Anonymous Donations Would Uphold Free Speech

No aspect of an anonymous system would stymie speech. Donors would be able to contribute gobs of cash to any political cause they wished to support. But because of mandated anonymity, they wouldn't get the pork-barrel payoffs that now come with making big donations. When politicians don't know the sources of cash, the importance of the ideas themselves increases.

Needless to say, donors will privately tell politicians that they have contributed. In fact, the incentive is so strong that plenty of people who haven't contributed will be motivated to lie and say that they have. But there will be no way for politicians to check. Never knowing for sure who is talking straight and who is double-dealing, our representatives would be forced back to the very rationale for free speech—the ideas and policies that they promised to represent and implement.

Better still, our representatives might even consider the common good. Secrecy in contributions would eliminate incentives to introduce favoritism into the tax code, appropriations bills or the vast regulatory system of the modern welfare state. Who knows what might happen when politicians no longer know how much the teachers unions are contributing?

If you think requiring anonymity for political donations wouldn't work or is impractical, ask yourself: Does the secret ballot work? Imagine politicians paying you if you promise to vote for them. You can't—for good reason. The secrecy of the voting booth prevents anyone from knowing whether you are true to your promise. The same would hold for an anonymous campaign finance system.

> *"The DISCLOSE Act ... was devised to cure the secrecy problem and provide disclosure of the contributors and the amounts they give."*

Full Disclosure of Political Donors Is the Best Way to Prevent Corruption

Fred Wertheimer

Fred Wertheimer is a campaign finance reform activist and president of the watchdog group Democracy 21. In the following viewpoint, the author argues that unlimited and undisclosed campaign contributions, particularly when funneled through tax-exempt organizations, can lead to systemic corruption that will only be addressed through passage of stricter disclosure laws. Wertheimer identifies the main problem as so-called shadow groups, set-up as 501(c)(4)s, which do not have to report their donors by law. According to Wertheimer, most of the shadow groups have been formed by operatives of the Republican National Committee including Karl Rove, the chief political advisor to former President George W. Bush. Wertheimer examines one list of contributors to one of Roves earlier 527 groups, finding that the primary donors consisted of American billionaires. Wert-

*heimer concludes that swift passage of the Democracy Is
Strengthened by Casting Light on Spending in Elections
(DISCLOSE) Act is the only way to curtail the corruption.*

As you read, consider the following questions:

1. What are the two main "shadow groups" of the Republican National Committee, according to the author?

2. How does Wertheimer assert that the US Chamber of Commerce will fund its 2010 campaign contributions?

3. According to Wertheimer, what percentage of voters favor disclosure legislation?

E ver since the 1972 Federal Election Campaign Act passed, public disclosure of the money used to influence elections has been a cardinal rule of U.S. politics.

Voters' right to know who is behind the money spent trying to sway them was firmly established by the Supreme Court's 1976 decision in *Buckley v. Valeo*, which upheld the constitutionality of campaign finance disclosure laws.

But now, secret money has returned to U.S. politics and is flooding the 2010 congressional races.

The main vehicles being used to hide donors are 501(c)(4) tax-exempt organizations, which do not have to disclose their donors. These groups are expected to spend tens of millions of dollars on the 2010 congressional races.

The Rise of 501(c)(4) and 527 Groups

Many news outlets have reported this year about the dire financial condition of the Republican National Committee [RNC], but this turns out to be an illusionary problem.

Two "shadow RNC" groups, American Crossroads GPS and American Action Network, are prime examples of full-scale political operations run inside the structure of tax-exempt 501(c)(4) groups. They were both set up this year by leading GOP [Republican] political operatives to elect Republicans in the midterm races. As 501(c)(4)'s, their activities are financed by contributors kept secret from the public.

These two groups, along with a third "shadow RNC" group, American Crossroads, a 527 political organization, have announced plans to spend at least $75 million in the 2010 congressional races. While American Crossroads, as a 527, has to disclose its donors, most campaign expenditures by these groups are expected to be made by the two 501(c)(4)s and financed with undisclosed contributions.

Trade associations also are being used to conceal donors financing campaign spending. The U.S. Chamber of Commerce, for example, is set to spend $75 million in the 2010 congressional races, funded by undisclosed contributors.

The Shadow RNC

The three shadow groups were formed by some of the top Republican political operatives—and are based in the same building.

Both American Crossroads and American Crossroads GPS were established by Karl Rove, former President George W. Bush's chief political adviser, and Ed Gillespie, a former RNC chairman.

The head of American Crossroads, Mike Duncan, is another former RNC chairman. He has said the two groups plan to spend nearly $50 million in 11 Senate races this year.

The third group, American Action Network, was formed by several other Republican leaders, including former Sen. Norm Coleman. The GOP fundraiser Fred Malek is a key player in the group, which announced plans to spend $25 million to support Republican congressional candidates this year.

The Center for Public Integrity recently reported that another 501(c)(4) shadow RNC group was being formed by Scott Reed, a Republican operative, who says "he's raised about half of the $25 million he's hoping to spend to influence a few Senate and 20 House contests." Reed did not disclose the group's name.

Rove and Gillespie first established American Crossroads as a 527 but then set up American Crossroads GPS as an affiliated 501(c)(4)—that does not disclose its donors and can therefore serve as a haven to hide big donors.

According to POLITICO, Steven Law, president of both groups, made clear that secrecy for donors was a key reason for establishing the 501(c)(4), saying, "I wouldn't want to discount the value of confidentiality to some donors."

As of Aug. 23, [2010] American Crossroads and American Crossroads GPS had raised a combined $17.6 million as of Aug. 23, with $6.5 million reported by the 527 group, and almost twice as much, or $11.1 million, reported by the 501(c)(4), according to the BNA [Bureau of National Affairs] *Money and Politics Report*.

Since the formation of the 501(c)(4), most contributions raised by the two groups have gone to the (c)(4)—where donors' identities are kept secret.

World's Billionaires Unite

The first contributions for the Rove/Gillespie operation were raised for American Crossroads, their 527, and had to be disclosed. Examining these contributions can offer some idea of the kind of donors for American Crossroads GPS, which does not disclose contributors.

The original donor of choice for American Crossroads was a billionaire. The original contribution of choice was $1 million.

According to POLITICO, *Salon* and the Center for Public Integrity, the initial donors to American Crossroads included:

- Billionaire Bradley Wayne Hughes, chairman of Public Storage Inc.—$1.55 million;

- Billionaire Trevor Rees-Jones, president of Dallas-based Chief Oil and Gas—$1 million;

- Billionaire Harold Simmons's company, Southwest Louisiana Land LLC—$1 million;

- Dixie Rice Agricultural Corp., in which billionaire Harold Simmons is a major investor—$1 million

- Billionaire Robert Rowling's company, TRT Holdings—$1 million;

- Billionaire Jerry Perenchio's Living Trust—$1 million.

The DISCLOSE Act

The explosion of secret money in the 2010 races was triggered by the Supreme Court's 5-4 decision in *Citizens United v. Federal Election Commission*, which struck down the long-standing ban on corporations making campaign expenditures to influence federal elections.

More than 75 percent of voters, including 70 percent of Republicans and 73 percent of independents, according to a recent Survey USA poll, view such corporate election spending as an attempt to bribe politicians rather than as free speech.

The *Citizens United* decision opened the door for 501(c)(4) advocacy groups and 501(c)(6) trade associations to make unlimited campaign expenditures funded by undisclosed contributions.

The DISCLOSE [Democracy Is Strengthened by Casting Light on Spending in Elections] Act, which passed the House in June, was devised to cure the secrecy problem and provide disclosure of the contributors and the amounts they give.

But the act was one vote short of getting to the Senate floor in July, when no Republican senator voted to allow the legislation to be considered. The bill is expected to come up for a vote again this month [September 2010].

While a new law cannot be passed in time to shed light on the secret funding of this year's races, passing the DISCLOSE Act in this Congress would restore to future federal elections the basic principle that voters have a right to know who is behind the money being spent to influence their votes.

Periodical Bibliography

The following articles have been selected to supplement the diverse views presented in this chapter.

Joan Aikens, Lee Ann Elliott, Thomas Josefiak, et al.	"Chuck Schumer vs. Free Speech," *Wall Street Journal*, May 19, 2010.
Nick Baumann	"Scott Brown and the DISCLOSE Act," *Mother Jones*, July 16, 2010.
Devin Dwyer	"Democrats Holster 'Disclose' Bill Facing NRA, Accusations of Double Standard," *ABC News*, June 21, 2010.
Warner Todd Huston	"Disclosure Act: Another Example of Unconstitutional Obamaism," *Chicago Now*, June 25, 2010.
Cleta Mitchell	"NRA Exemption Shows Campaign Disclosure Bill's Cynical, Fatal Flaws," *Washington Post*, June 17, 2010.
David A. Patten	"U.S. Chamber Official: DISCLOSE Act 'Shreds' Constitution," Newsmax.com, July 25, 2010.
Ted Roelofs	"Sketchy Groups, Secret Donors Use New Campaign Finance Ruling to Sway Political Campaigns," *Grand Rapids Press*, October 17, 2010.
Paul S. Ryan	"*Citizens United* and the 'Effective Disclosure' System That Wasn't," *Campaign Legal Center*, January 24, 2011.
John Samples	"The DISCLOSE Act, Deliberation, and the First Amendment," *Policy Analysis*, June 28, 2010.
Nikki Willoughby	"DISCLOSE Act Is an Opening, Not a Barrier," *Cato Unbound*, November 12, 2010.

CHAPTER 2

How Would Publicly Funded Elections Change the Campaign Process?

Chapter Preface

Political corruption is a fact of life in almost any governing system. In 1792, French revolutionary Louis Antoine Léon de Saint-Just said, "It is never possible to rule innocently." Public funding of elections was intended to lend balance to the process so politicians would not be beholden to wealthy contributors and to make it easier for more candidates to enter races, thus increasing competition. Whether or not the seven US states that have adopted "clean elections," as they are known, have experienced an improvement in the way their political campaigns are run is debatable, but some of the scandals prior to the movement to adopt public funding for political races were severe enough to convince many voters that something had to be done.

Residents of Arizona voted in favor of clean elections in 1998, after one of the state's worst periods of political scandal, known as AzScam or "Operation Desert Sting." Suspecting that lawmakers were accepting bribes in return for favors on a proposed casino deal, the district attorney's office in Phoenix tapped a former Mafia associate from Las Vegas named Joseph Stedino to go undercover as "Tony Vincent" and offer bribes to Arizona politicians and lobbyists. Stedino published a book in 1992 about his experience as an undercover agent in the AzScam bust—*What's in It for Me? How an Ex-Wiseguy Exposed the Greed, Jealousy, and Lust that Drive Arizona Politics*, written with journalist Dary Matera. Stedino encountered so many Arizona politicians who were on the take, lobbyists willing to "rub out" other lobbyists, and other examples of sleaze and corruption that local law enforcement officials allegedly wondered who would be left to run the state after all the indictments were handed out. According to Robert Barnes, writing for the *Washington Post* in 2010, "At one point, 10 percent of the Arizona legislature faced civil or criminal charges related to the scandal." Reviewing the book for the *San Diego Union-Tribune*, Philip J. LaVelle observed, "After reading *What's in It for Me?* it's reasonable to wonder whether Arizonans would be better off without a state government."

In response to AzScam, Arizonans voted in favor of clean elections in a 1998 referendum. But even that legislation has been controversial, due to a matching funds clause that provides additional money to publicly funded candidates once their independently funded opponents reach a certain level of fundraising. In theory, this provision is intended to level the field so that all candidates have an equal chance of winning an election. But critics point out that in practice it causes candidates who opt to fund their campaigns without public money to avoid adequate fundraising because they know their own fundraising will trigger the state to provide more money for their political foes. Opponents of the system believe this tendency to delay fundraising has the effect of inhibiting the free speech of independently funded candidates. As of early 2011, the Supreme Court had agreed to hear the case *McComish v. Bennett*, which challenges the matching funds provision on First Amendment grounds. In light of the court's January 2010 decision in *Citizens United v. Federal Election Commission*—which granted First Amendment protection to corporations and nonprofit organizations in allowing them to make unlimited political contributions from their corporate treasuries—many commentators expect the court to strike down the Arizona matching funds clause. This in turn would weaken the case for publicly funded elections across the country. Loyola Law School professor and campaign finance expert Richard L. Hasen wrote about the situation on the Loyola Law School blog on November 28, 2010: "[R]ational politicians who are serious candidates will not opt into the public financing plan unless they think they will be able to run a competitive campaign under the public financing system. The whole point of the extra matching funds in the Arizona plan is to give candidates assurance they won't be vastly outspent in their election. While an adverse ruling by the Supreme Court in *McComish* would not mean that *all* public financing systems would be unconstitutional, it would eliminate one of the best ways to create *effective* public financing systems."

The viewpoints in the following chapter examine the debate over public funding of elections, including whether publicly funded elections reduce or increase free speech and corruption, as well as judicial neutrality.

> *"As the Supreme Court concludes its deliberations on the role of corporate spending in federal elections, it is time to pursue a new and affirmative course in campaign finance reform."*

Public Election Funding Enhances the Free Speech of Candidates and Voters

Daniel Weeks

Daniel Weeks is president of Americans for Campaign Reform. In the following viewpoint, Weeks includes publicly funded elections systems among a number of reforms that would address issues of accountability and flexibility for political candidates and public officeholders. Weeks specifically advocates for the passage of the Fair Elections Now Act, which would encourage small donors and provide matching public funds. After reviewing campaign finance legislation and Supreme Court decisions since the 1976 ruling in Buckley v. Valeo, *Weeks suggests the* Citizens United v. Federal Election Commission *case represents the ultimate challenge to campaign finance reform. The answer, he maintains, is the Fair Elections Now Act, which will reconcile free speech with donor transparency while ensuring that candidates remain accountable to the public.*

As you read, consider the following questions:

1. What three problems are cited by the author as arguments for greater government oversight of campaign spending?

2. According to the author, what are the two "complementary" components of successful campaign finance reform?

3. How does Weeks describe the "public accountability frame"?

Difficult though it may be to imagine American politics unconstrained by big money in elections, that is hardly reason for pragmatic progressives not to think creatively about the sources, uses, and effects of private campaign cash. For those concerned about the distribution of political voice and power in our democracy—not to mention the nation's ability to address an ominous set of economic, social, and environmental challenges—it may be the most important long-term question we face. And with the Supreme Court set to hand down a landmark decision in *Citizens United v. Federal Election Commission* on the "free speech" rights of corporations to spend unlimited sums of money on political campaigns, the time for Congress to reconsider this question is now.

The Old Frame: Regulate and Restrict

Money in American elections is hardly a novel concern. Since the days of Theodore Roosevelt, reformers have sought to counter the corrupting influence of private wealth in public elections. While the playing field has changed since the turn of the 20th century, the debate has remained much the same.

Liberals have traditionally sought to regulate and restrict the flow of money in elections. To many, private contributions to candidates for public office are inherently problematic. Political donors, the thinking goes, are predominantly motivated by a desire for particularistic gain, while politicians willingly indulge at taxpayer expense. Political corruption, lack of electoral competition, and public disenchantment with government are cited as reasons for increased government oversight of campaign money; lower contribution limits, caps on campaign spending, and increased regulation of independent expenditures have been among the favored responses to counter these problems. The emerging role of small donations from a rapidly expanding base of middle-income Americans who scarcely conform to the "special interest" mold has only begun to change this mindset.

By contrast, conservatives have staunchly objected to regulation of any kind in the name of free and unfettered debate. They favor disclosure of campaign contributions as an alternative to government-imposed limits: let the public know the sources of political money and it will act as it sees fit. Many argue that less regulation, not more, will free politicians from the cumbersome task of dialing for special-interest dollars and enable outsiders (albeit those with access to wealth) to more effectively compete.

The U.S. Supreme Court, for its part, has endeavored to strike a balance between the reformist call for government regulation and conservative opposition in the name of freedom of speech. In a landmark 1976 ruling in *Buckley v. Valeo*, the Supreme Court held that spending money on political campaigns was subject to full First Amendment protection as free (if you can afford it) speech. Contributing money to campaigns, by contrast, was held to be an indirect form of political speech subject to reasonable limits in the interest of preventing corruption—or the appearance of it—in government. (The limit was set at $1,000 per contribution in 1976; it is at $2,400 today.) Subsequent Supreme Court cases have upheld the right of individuals to influence elections through independent spending, while limits on corporate and labor union spending have thus far been maintained.

In each of four major legislative landmarks in campaign reform over the last century, liberals have succeeded at gradually extending government regulation over the sources and sums of political cash. Important as each reform has been in incrementally righting wrongs, few on the right or left today would deny that our campaign finance system leaves much to be desired. A new, more affirmative approach to the role of money in elections is badly needed.

The "More Speech" Answer to a Conservative Supreme Court

A generation after the Supreme Court's controversial *Buckley* ruling equating money and freedom of speech, the Court is again testing the constitutional limits of government regulation of our campaign finance system. At issue in the present *Citizens United v. Federal Election Commission* case is whether corporations and labor unions—in this case, the corporate-backed Citizens United organization, producer of 2008's *Hillary: The Movie*—can spend from their treasuries to influence the outcome of elections. At stake is more than a century of campaign finance laws.

Once again the two camps have assembled, one to assert that restricting corporate and labor union is necessary to prevent corruption, and the other to demand that First Amendment rights be universally extended to all, individuals and corporations alike. But there is a false assumption at the center of this debate. Government regulation and freedom of speech are not necessarily at odds when it comes to the role of money in American elections. The question is not *whether* we should regulate the transfer of private wealth between those with a vested interest in government policy and the public officials who make and enforce such policy (it does not take a constitutional lawyer to recognize the conflict of interest). Instead, it is *how* to fashion campaign finance laws so they meaningfully advance the legitimate aims of both sides: preventing corruption and expanding freedom of speech.

Positively constructed campaign finance regulation and freedom of political speech are both necessary and complementary components of a democratic campaign finance system. When government regulation is harnessed for the purpose of leveling up rather than limiting down the range and sum total of political speech, the result is a maximization of First Amendment rights. As laid out in the Fair Elections Now Act, a "more speech" solution would be predicated on encouraging broad-based small donations and matching public funds. It's an approach that recognizes that entering the political debate is a costly affair in our modern media environment, and that there is an uneven distribution of economic resources among citizens who seek to exercise First Amendment rights in campaigns. Further, it recognizes that political speech is not a zero-sum game, in which one person's spending diminishes another's ability to be heard. Empirical studies of the relationship between campaign spending and election outcomes have long shown that money matters *to a point*: candidates may lose for lack of adequate funds, but spending beyond a reasonable competitive threshold does not meaningfully affect the outcome.

As a result, when highly qualified candidates have access to sufficient campaign funding to make their message heard, there is little need to limit the spending of independently wealthy candidates or outside groups. In other words, let the wealthy speak—so long as theirs are not the only voices that ring out from the political arena. Such a leveling-up approach to campaign finance reform has been upheld as fully constitutional by the Supreme Court. Broadening the base of campaign funding to better reflect the public will and prevent conflicts of interest, the program does not replace—and, in fact, reinforces—common-sense regulations limiting the ability of corporations and unions to influence campaigns.

Focusing on System-Level Accountability

Like the debate over freedom of political speech, concerns over corruption and public accountability have unnecessarily divided advocates and opponents of campaign finance reform. Reformers have traditionally invoked the specter of government under the malign influence of "big money" as a chief motivation for reform. All politics, the theory goes, is corrupt and the only solution is to remove all links between special interests and public servants. Besides the obvious limitations of this account, the corruption frame prevents a rational assessment of the problem and reduces the range of policy tools with which we may respond.

The usual rebuttal to the corruption thesis centers on a contestation of the facts and the nature of political corruption. Opponents argue that instances of corruption are isolated and rare, and, when they do occur, are met with appropriate sanction under existing law. In other words, while a few bad apples are bound to turn up now and then, the electoral system itself is sound, and any measures extending beyond existing disclosure requirements and anti-bribery laws are excessive. That no amount of campaign finance regulation in the last 100 years has succeeded in completely eradicating corruption is taken to support the case.

A more constructive account on which to base reform moves from a focus on individual instances of corruption to a positive appeal for system-level accountability. It stresses the limitations and contradictions that are inherent in the campaign finance system and makes those deficiencies, rather than individual officeholders, the target of reform. Even while the corruption card has at times proven to be a powerful motivator of public support, a more nuanced and system-centered

Voter-Owned Elections Deliver Good Results

Studies by advocacy groups, the U.S. Government Accountability Office, state study commissions, and academic experts have concluded that the following positive outcomes can be expected from publicly funded elections:

- Candidate participation will increase as the system matures.

- Candidates will be generally pleased at having more time to meet with voters to collect qualifying contributions and discuss issues.

- The availability of public financing will attract candidates who might not otherwise run for office, especially women and minorities.

- Running as a "clean" candidate may be an advantage in open-seat races and occasionally against incumbents.

- More challengers will compete against incumbents in general elections, reducing the number of uncontested races and giving voters more choices.

Philip G. Rogers, Carl W. Stenberg, and Sarah J. Waterman,
"Voter-Owned Elections In North Carolina:
Public Financing of Campaigns,"
Popular Government, *Winter 2009.*

public accountability frame provides a more honest assessment of the facts and a stronger basis for reform.

According to this account, the problem does not lie in isolated cases of outright *quid pro quo* but rather in a *system* that actively encourages—even requires—unaccountable behavior on the part of elected officials in order to win and keep their seats. Front and center is the inherent contradiction in allowing society's regulators to finance their campaigns in large part through contributions from the very individuals and groups they are charged with regulating. Estimates of the economic cost of this system, if one considers only those spending programs that directly benefit major campaign contributors, run in the tens of billions of dollars per year. The larger economic cost of private campaign funding, in terms of increased rent-seeking and countless other market inefficiencies, are difficult to estimate but are a cause for grave concern. In the words of Rep. Barney Frank (D-MA), "Politicians are the only human beings in the world who are expected to take thousands of dollars from perfect strangers on important matters and not be affected by it."

The public accountability frame argues for a more nuanced examination of the role of money in politics. It identifies the legally sanctioned means by which "investor contributors" work within the existing system to limit the policy debate and ensure their interests are met. It questions whether politicians can effectively serve the interests of citizens when the need to raise campaign funds consumes an ever-increasing share of their time, and when the individuals with whom they interact in the fundraising process are scarcely representative of their constituents. And it enables a more productive collaboration between all parties involved by acknowledging the full scope of the challenge and withholding undue blame. In so doing, it enables a solution to the "corruption" problem that selectively preserves those elements of the current system (e.g. independent campaign spending) that are not at fault, and seeks to reform the rest.

A Small Donor Approach to Federal Campaign Finance

A retooled system of voluntary public funding of qualified candidates running for federal office—combining broad-based small donations with matching public funds—provides a viable alternative to private campaign funding in Congress today. The bipartisan Fair Elections Now Act would replace large donations from wealthy individuals and groups with donations of no more than $100 per contributor raised from a candidate's constituents. Candidates seeking to participate in the voluntary program would be required to first raise at least 1,500 checks in amounts of $100 or less from within their home state. Once qualified, they would receive a four-dollars-to-one public match on every small donation they raise from their constituents, up to a competitive spending threshold. Once the threshold is reached, candidates are permitted to raise unlimited small donations without the benefit of public matching funds.

Under such a citizen-funding program, candidates who choose not to participate would remain free to raise and spend their private money on political speech under existing law. Independent groups would likewise be permitted to enter the political debate on their own terms. But history and common sense tell us that speech in a democratic society is not free when only the rich are heard. Cherishing the First Amendment requires that we extend speech opportunities to qualified candidates for public office irrespective of wealth. As noted above, for candidates with access to *sufficient* funding to make their message known to the voters, additional spending by themselves or their opponents has little determining effect.

As experience with citizen funding in seven states and more than a dozen cities from Arizona and Los Angeles to New York City and Maine has shown, large majorities of candidates willingly forego the big-money game—and the countless fundraising hours it demands—when presented with a small-donor alternative and matching public funds. More than three-quarters of candidates across the several states that have such systems are voluntarily opting in to citizen-funding programs and spending more time with the voters they seek to represent. Participation from small donors has increased several-fold and more candidates from diverse backgrounds are stepping forward to run for public office. Once in office, public officials report a new and welcome sense of independence to consider the full range of perspectives on policy matters put forward by interest groups and their constituents at large.

As a case in point, the state of Maine has seen candidate and small-donor participation in its program (called the Maine Clean Election Act) rise with each successive election since its inception in 2000. In 2008, more than 80 percent of candidates voluntarily opted in, compared with one-third in 2000, including more women candidates and candidates from diverse economic and professional backgrounds. As the rate of electoral competition has steadily increased—uncontested races are increasingly a thing of the past and incumbent re-election rates are down—the cost of running for office has markedly, if counterintuitively, declined. With thousands of Maine citizens becoming stakeholders in political campaigns through their small donations, the rate of voter turnout in Maine has increased with each election, making it among the highest in the nation today.

In a 2007 study by the Maine Commission on Governmental Ethics and Election Practices, lawmaker and candidate responses to the public-funding system were enthusiastic. Among the representative remarks from respondents included, "I like the statement it makes . . . that I am not beholden to lobbying organizations and major donors," "[I] don't want to feel beholden to anyone but my constituents," and "I believe Clean Elections have improved Maine's responsiveness to citizens and reduced the influence of lobbyists."

As the Supreme Court concludes its deliberations on the role of corporate spending in federal elections, it is time to pursue a new and affirmative course in campaign finance reform. Members of Congress concerned with the ability of government to meet the considerable challenges facing the nation today would do well to join the more than 120 of their colleagues from both sides of the aisle who have already stood up for citizen-funded elections. Respect for the constitutional principles of fairness and freedom of speech demands nothing less.

*"Public funding is a program that prom-
ises much, delivers little, and raises real
constitutional and policy problems."*

Publicly Funded Elections Infringe on Candidates' First Amendment Rights

David M. Primo

*David M. Primo is associate professor of political science at the
University of Rochester, in Rochester, New York. In the following
viewpoint, Primo presents research demonstrating that public
funding of candidates adversely affects the campaign process, in-
hibits the free speech of privately funded candidates, and has
little or no effect on voter participation. Primo cites research that
indicates that independently funded candidates in Arizona whose
opponents are publicly funded tended to delay their own fundraising to avoid triggering the state's matching funds clause. In
addition, Primo argues that public funding of elections produces
no significant difference in the way the public views candidates,
nor does it appear to alter the amount of corruption in politics.*

As you read, consider the following questions:

1. How has public funding affected voter perceptions of government, according to Primo?

2. Acording to the author, does public funding tend to increase or decrease voter turnout?

3. The US Government Accountability Office (GAO) surveyed the voters of which states that have publicly funded elections systems?

The issue of public funding for political campaigns is heating up as the U.S. Supreme Court considers whether to take up the case of *Arizona Freedom Club PAC [political action committee] v. Bennett,* a First Amendment challenge by the Institute for Justice to Arizona's public funding law. Legal challenges to similar laws in Connecticut and Florida continue to work their way through the courts, and the U.S. Congress is considering the Fair Elections Now Act, which would provide congressional candidates with government money to run for office. Public funding advocates often make bold claims about the benefits of these systems, but scientific evidence supporting these claims is scarce. This research brief examines the evidence about the effects of public funding.

1. Do "matching funds"—the focus of Arizona Freedom Club PAC v. Bennett—*have an effect on the speech of independent groups and candidates who refuse to accept government subsidies?*

Yes, matching funds cause candidates to alter the timing of their speech in campaigns, infringing First Amendment rights.

Arizona's public funding system, known as "Clean Elections," provides additional public subsidies—so-called "matching funds"—to publicly funded candidates whenever their privately funded opponents or independent groups raise or spend more than a limit set by the government. For example, in a multi-member House race, once a privately funded candidate has raised or spent up to the government cap, every additional dollar he raises for or spends on his own speech results in an additional dollar of matching funds for *all* of his publicly funded opponents (minus 6 percent to account for fundraising costs). Moreover, if a group independent of the privately funded candidate spends money speaking out in his favor, his publicly funded opponents are again entitled to matching funds. In effect, then, when independent groups or privately funded candidates speak in amounts deemed excessive by the government, the government attempts to "level" that speech by directly subsidizing their political and ideological opponents. Those challenging the law in *Arizona Freedom Club PAC* argue that matching funds unconstitutionally burden the speech of independent groups and candidates who refuse public funds for their campaigns.

The only statistical research on the effects of matching funds on candidate speech shows that many privately supported candidates facing the prospect of triggering matching funds for their opponents alter the timing of their speech as a result. Specifically, Arizona candidates at risk of triggering matching funds delay their fundraising and spending until the last possible minute in a campaign, holding fire in order to postpone the distribution of matching funds and make them less useful to opponents. Late fundraising and spending of candidates facing the prospect of matching funds far outstrips that of other privately funded candidates *not* threatened by matching funds by four to one in the two weeks before Arizona House primary campaigns and, in competitive races, by three to one in the two weeks before the general election. This demonstrates that candidates are acting to minimize the harm caused to their campaigns by their own speech as a result of matching funds distributed under Arizona's "Clean Elections" act.

For a May 2010 review of Clean Elections programs, the General Accounting Office interviewed candidates and independent groups who also said that to avoid triggering matching funds, independent groups and privately supported candidates delay raising and spending money on speech until late in the campaign. Indeed, earlier research by political scientist Michael Miller shows that this now is common practice in Arizona. Every single privately funded candidate he surveyed raised concerns about matching funds, and some informed Miller that they put off spending until the last minute to avoid helping the opposition with matching funds. As one privately funded candidate put it, "Every dollar I spend over the threshold starts feeding the alligator trying to eat me ... I sent out a lot less mail and held a lot less events than I would have but for my hands feeling like they were tied under this systems."

Questions About the Effects of Public Funding

2. Does public funding improve citizen perceptions of government?

The only statistical study to examine the effect of state public funding laws on perceptions of government found that public funding has, in some cases, a small negative effect.

Reformers often claim that replacing private voluntary donations to campaigns with public funding will "clean up" politics. If so, we would expect that citizen perceptions of government would improve as a result. However, in the only study to statistically examine the effect of state public funding laws on perceptions of government, my co-author, Jeffrey Milyo, and I demonstrate that these laws had a small, but negative, effect. We examined survey questions asking citizens whether they believed that they had a say in what government does, whether public officials care about what people like them think and whether they find politics complicated. After controlling for individual- and state-level factors that could muddy the findings, we demonstrate that citizens in states with public funding programs were *less* likely to believe that officials care what people like them think and *less* likely to believe that they had a say in what government does.

The small negative effects may be due to the fact that public funding programs rarely live up to the expectations set by reformers. When few positive effects of "better" elections or policymaking materialize, this may lead to increased disillusionment or, at best, have a neutral effect on perceptions of government. Moreover, the effects may be negligible because many voters are not even aware of the laws. More than a decade ago, Maine and Arizona enacted one type of public funding system, Clean Elections programs that prohibit participating candidates from receiving private contributions in exchange for full public funding. Yet in a recent survey conducted by the GAO [Government Accountability Office], barely half of the respondents in those two states were even "a little aware" of these laws. And, of those in Maine who were aware of the laws, only 20 percent said the laws increased their confidence in government, while 15 percent said the laws decreased their confidence in government. The comparable figures in Arizona were 26 percent and 22 percent. The rest were unsure or said Clean Elections laws had no effect.

3. Does public funding affect voter participation?

The strongest evidence shows that public funding has no effect on or reduces *voter turnout.*

The most rigorous examination of this question to date studied turnout in all 50 states, controlling for a variety of factors that could affect turnout rates, In a working paper, two co-authors and I find no effect of public funding (both full- and partial-funding systems) on turnout in gubernatorial elections and a modestly negative effect on turnout in legislative elections. Looking specifically at Clean Elections systems for legislative candidates, we estimate that they lead to a *reduction* in turnout of about two percent.

In another working paper, Miller studies Clean Elections in Maine and Connecticut and shows that voters who have *already* turned out to vote are more likely to cast a vote in a legislative race (rather than abstaining from that particular race) if at least one of the candidates has accepted public funds. Miller does not suggest that more voters are heading to the polls as a result of Clean Elections, only that fewer voters are failing to cast votes in certain races, and this effect is small—a 1.5 to 2 percentage point reduction in such ballot "roll-off." In fact, Miller focuses on roll-off in part because he does not expect that public funding of state legislative races will affect turnout: "Even in the fully funded state legislative elections, it is unrealistic to assume that down-ticket races alone can affect the number of citizens who turn out to vote."

The results of previous research on public funding and turnout, which had methodological limitations, are mixed. The strongest evidence, therefore, points to public funding at best having a tiny positive effect in reducing roll-off, and at worst having a negative effect on turnout overall.

There are at least two reasons why public funding may not increase turnout, as reformers promise. First, public funding programs may depress turnout indirectly: When the promised effects on policymaking are not borne out, trust in government and citizens' beliefs that they can make a difference are depressed, in turn lowering turnout. Second, public funding may lead to spending reductions in competitive races, which may depress turnout compared to a privately funded campaign. Further research is necessary to examine these possibilities.

4. Does public funding increase the competitiveness of elections?

There is no consistent body of scholarly research establishing that public funding increases campaign competitiveness.

Some measures of electoral competitiveness increased after Arizona and Maine implemented Clean Elections programs—

but it is not clear that Clean Elections was the cause. Furthermore, although some measures of electoral competitiveness increased, this was not the case for all or even the most important measurements.

For example, studies show that Maine saw more candidates running for office and Arizona saw more contested races (those where candidates have opponents) after reform. This is not surprising: One of the basic principles of economics is that if you subsidize something, you get more of it. Pay politicians to run for office and more will. Data also suggest that there are more races with narrow vote margins. But the same data show that incumbents are reelected just about as often after reform as before, so challengers are no more successful at gaining office, contrary to reformers' hopes. Indeed, one study concludes that the 2004 House election in Arizona was "something of a disappointment to campaign finance reformers: The percentage of incumbents in competitive races in 2004 was the same as it was in 2000 (about 36 percent), declining from a post-1990 record of 47 percent in 2002." Although such before-and-after snapshots are instructive, it is very difficult to determine whether Clean Elections caused these changes. Other factors may be at play, and these studies do not attempt to account for them. For example, during the same time period, Maine changed contribution limits in significant ways, and Arizona implemented term limits.

So what do statistical studies that do attempt to control for such complicating factors show? Overall, there is limited evidence that either Clean Elections or other public funding programs that offer only partial funding have appreciably affected competitiveness, if we focus on measures like narrow vote margin or reelection rates. For example, two co-authors and I find little effect of public funding programs on competitiveness in gubernatorial elections and note that the modest positive effects of the laws on legislative elections, as identified by other authors, are likely to dissipate over time due to candidates strategically adjusting to the law, among other factors. Political scientist Neil Malhotra finds that Clean Elections had some pro-competitive effects in the 2000 Arizona Senate election, but his approach has some methodological limitations. For instance, Malhotra uses only one year of data during which the Clean Elections law was in force—the first year, 2000—so we do not know if these results are part of a pattern or apply only to 2000. Economist Thomas Stratmann, in a study of 42 states, estimates that partial public funding in Minnesota and Clean Elections in Maine reduce vote margins dramatically (by 15 percentage points) but have no effect on incumbent reelection rates. However, Stratmann does not control for unobserved or immeasurable factors in the states that may drive vote margins, such as the pool of quality candidates, so these results may be tapping more than the effect of public funding. Finally, the GAO study finds no evidence that incumbent reelection rates in Maine and Arizona were affected by Clean Elections. Moreover, although the GAO determined that vote margins appeared to decrease in recent years, they were not able to attribute those declines to Clean Elections.

5. Does public funding reduce the perception or reality of "special interest" influence in politics? What about corruption?

Survey and interview evidence does not support the claim that special interest influence has been reduced in politics.

The aforementioned GAO survey asked Maine and Arizona residents whether they believed Clean Elections has reduced special interest influence. About the same percentage of respondents believed that interest group influence had *increased*—17 percent in Maine and 24 percent in Arizona—as believed it had *decreased*—19 percent in Maine and 25 percent in Arizona. The GAO also interviewed 11 candidates for office in both Maine and Arizona and asked them about their perceptions of the role of interests in the wake of Clean Elections. In Maine, only four candidates believed interest group influence had decreased, and all of these were publicly funded candidates. In Arizona, only two candidates believed this to be the case. Results for interviews with interest groups were not markedly different.

For political scientists and economists, these results are not surprising. First, there is very little systematic evidence that campaign contributions affect the decisions of elected officials. Groups may have many motivations for giving, but it is not realistic to think that an elected official will change his or her vote on a piece of legislation based on a small contribution. In fact, if it were the case that money could move votes, corporate political action committees (PACs) would presumably max out their contributions to elected officials each year. Yet, corporate PACs rarely hit donation ceilings at the federal level. Second, campaign contributions are only one way that interests can participate in the political process. Lobbying, for instance, is an important way that interest groups transmit information about the likely consequences of legislation. Even legislators elected through Clean Elections receive this information.

Public Funding Programs Offer Few Benefits

As Congress considers the Fair Elections Now Act and the U.S. Supreme Court decides whether to hear *Arizona Freedom Club PAC v. Bennett* on the merits of matching funds, public debate will focus on questions about the effects of public funding systems and claims that they improve perceptions of government, encourage competitiveness in electoral races, and encourage participation in the political process. In answering these questions, the importance of social scientific evidence is paramount. While statistical evidence is never perfect and should be rigorously scrutinized, it is important that the best evidence be brought to bear on questions that speak to fundamental First Amendment concerns.

Comparing the claims and promises made by public funding advocates with the actual evidence demonstrates that public funding programs have delivered few, if any, of the benefits promised by their promoters, and they have certainly not resulted in the fundamental transformation and rebirth of confidence in government the promoters sought. On the other hand, the cost of such programs—not only in terms of their negative effect on the timing and nature of political speech in the states with such programs, but also in terms of wasted public resources—has been demonstrable and real. In other words, public funding is a program that promises much, delivers little, and raises real constitutional and policy problems.

> *"Money is compromising the appearance, if the not the reality, of judicial impartiality, the bedrock foundation of our court system."*

Public Funding of Elections Would Ensure Judicial Neutrality

William R. Andersen

William R. Andersen is Judson Falknor Professor of Law Emeritus at the University of Washington's School of Law. In the following viewpoint, Andersen favors publicly funded judicial elections because funding would then be open to all candidates and would encourage challengers to incumbents, thus enhancing political participation. Andersen maintains that public funding of judicial elections would ensure neutrality among judges because it virtually eliminates special interest money from elections. According to Andersen, the role of judges in society is to interpret the law and resolve conflicts with as much neutrality as possible, and the presence of money in judicial elections has a computing effect.

As you read, consider the following questions:

1. Which Washington State representative introduced House Bill 1186?

2. According to Andersen, has public funding of judicial elections generally been partisan or bipartisan?

3. According to the author, would public funding of judicial elections encourage or discourage challengers to incumbent judges?

The problem is not hard to state:

- We all want fair and impartial courts—in a free society, the very concept of the rule of law requires judges who are impartial, objective, disinterested and unbiased, but;

- Poll after poll has told us what common sense confirms: that when elected judges are seen as beholden to large campaign contributors, both the reality and the appearance of impartiality can suffer, and;

- Large campaign contributions are escalating dramatically in [the state of] Washington's judicial elections. They almost quadrupled in 2006, and, as we all remember, most of the increase seems to have been used for highly personal attack ads which conveyed little if any relevant information to voters.

Public Funding Encourages Judicial Neutrality

The problem is obvious—money is compromising the appearance, if not the reality, of judicial impartiality, the bedrock foundation of our court system. Our Legislature has begun to respond.

Rep. Shay Schual-Berke, D-Normandy Park, and others have introduced House Bill 1186, which would provide for a six-year pilot program for public funding of state Supreme Court and Court of Appeals elections for any judicial candidate who could show substantial support for his or her campaign and who would agree not to spend beyond the funds provided. The level of public funding is set at about the traditional (pre-2006) cost of judicial election campaigns.

This is not a new idea. Several other states provide public funding for elections, and where it has been used for judicial elections the results have been impressive. Public financing is entirely voluntary and it is available for any qualifying candidate who agrees to the limitations on campaign expenditures.

Public financing is also entirely neutral—it has been used by conservatives and liberals, men and women, minority candidates, incumbents and challengers. It has successfully reduced the flow of special-interest money into elections.

"Judges Are Not Legislators"

Still, the idea of public funding has its critics. Some say that an impartial judicial system is simply not possible—that courts are political institutions and can never be impartial. That argument dangerously misunderstands the role of law in a free society. It is imperative to appreciate that judges are not legislators. We want and expect our legislators to be blessed in favor of voter preferences. That is democracy.

But the judge's role is quite different. The judge's job is to resolve conflicts in the interpretation and application of laws enacted by the Legislature. Judges have limited policy-making authority and even that is never final. Legislators (or the people) are always free to rewrite a law if they believe a judicial interpretation is wrong.

Properly viewed, the judge's narrower job is impartial conflict resolution. We must protect that impartiality, the fairness it provides and the public confidence it inspires.

No System Is Perfect

Still others say that public funding will entrench incumbents and thus be unfair to challengers. To the contrary, in other states publicly financed challengers have defeated incumbents. Common sense suggests that public funding would benefit many challengers, since they are not likely to have a history of contacts with major funding sources. To many otherwise qualified challengers, public support will be a welcome admission ticket into the arena.

While this plan has been carefully designed, the concept is new to Washington and there are the usual uncertainties. But no change is risk-free, and solving real problems is seldom accomplished by waiting for perfection.

We need to get our relative priorities in order, to understand that some things (and some arguments) are more important than others, and to appreciate that now and then we have to accept some change in the status quo as the price of accomplishing our most important goals. Ensuring our citizens the fairest and most impartial judicial system possible is just such a goal.

> "When government tells us what we must say ... it must have a compelling interest in doing so, and it must adopt the least restrictive means available. To fund judicial elections with tax dollars satisfies neither criterion."

Publicly Funded Elections Would Not Eliminate Judicial Bias

Robert A. Levy

Robert A. Levy is chairman of the board of directors at the Cato Institute. He also sits on the boards of the Federalist Society, the Institute for Justice, and George Mason University School of Law. In the following viewpoint, Levy admits there are problems with the process of judicial elections, but he maintains that public funding would be prohibitively expensive, would inhibit challengers from running against incumbents, and would be a redundant effort to curb corruption because judges already are subject to ample ethical review. Although judges are indeed held to a different standard from other elected officials, namely in the assumption that their job is not to represent anyone's interest but instead to uphold the rule of law and to decide cases with im-

Robert A. Levy, "Public Funding for Judicial Elections: Forget It," Cato Institute, August 13, 2001. Copyright © by The Cato Institute. Reproduced by permission.

partiality, Levy argues that proposals to institute a public funding system for judicial elections will favor fringe candidates over serious ones and present numerous oversight difficulties regarding cost.

As you read, consider the following questions:

1. In what way, according to the author, does public funding of judicial elections favor incumbents?

2. What is it that "sustains publicly funded elections," according to Levy?

3. Name some of the ethical standards and requirements to which judges are subject that legislators are not, as noted in the viewpoint.

At its meeting in Chicago this month [August 2001], the American Bar Association [ABA] unveiled the recommendations of its Commission on Public Financing of Judicial Campaigns. The Commission, allegedly concerned about "inappropriate politicization of the judiciary," has urged that contested elections for state supreme court justices and some appellate judges be publicly funded. Ironically, that proposal will be embraced by the same association of 400,000 lawyers and judges most responsible for politicizing the profession it purports to represent. The ABA officially promotes a liberal agenda on issues ranging from federal gun control to affirmative action to universal health care.

The real goal of the new financing scheme isn't as lofty as the Commission contends. Instead, we are witnessing the opening salvo in a crusade to publicly fund federal and state elections for all three branches of government.

There may be good arguments for merit selection of judges followed by periodic, unopposed retention elections. But contested elections raise serious questions. They've become inordinately expensive, create a perception of impropriety, and may produce judges beholden to deep-pocketed donors with recurring business before the court. While politicians are expected to fight for their constituents, judges are supposed to have an allegiance to the rule of law, not to individual or corporate interests. Still, voters in many states have resisted attempts to replace judicial elections with executive appointments. That's the problem the ABA Commission claims to address. Lamentably, the proposed cure is worse than the disease.

Publicly Funded Judicial Elections Have Serious Drawbacks

Public funding favors current office-holders by denying to challengers the financial resources needed to overcome the advantages of incumbency. Public Funding is opposed by taxpayers; just look at the small percentage who have opted to check off tax dollars for presidential campaigns. Ordinarily, public funding is tied to prior vote counts or fundraising, thereby penalizing new candidates. Without those ties, however, public funding diverts resources to fringe candidates. The Commission blithely wishes away that problem by asserting that only "serious" candidates will receive money. Yet our experience with presidential elections isn't encouraging. Big bucks have fattened the campaign coffers of luminaries like ultra-leftist Lenora Fulani and convicted felon Lyndon LaRouche.

Naturally, there's the issue of cost, about which the Commission professes no insight and offers no solution. And finally, of paramount importance, there's the moral and constitutional concern over coerced speech. "To compel a man to furnish contributions of money for the propagation of opinions which he disbelieves and abhors," said Thomas Jefferson, "is sinful and tyrannical." Yes it is. But coerced speech is what sustains publicly funded elections. When government tells us what we must say—abridging core rights guaranteed by the

First Amendment—it must have a compelling interest in doing so, and it must adopt the least restrictive means available. To fund judicial elections with tax dollars satisfies neither criterion.

Judges Already Are Subject to Standards

Presumably, the compelling state interest is the same for judges as for legislators—to avoid actual or apparent corruption. Then again, the community is much better protected from venal judges than from shady lawmakers. Judges deal with concrete cases in which the interests of the attorneys and the litigants are unmistakable, thus ripe for public scrutiny. Similarly, the judge's link to the outcome of the case is unambiguous. Judges are usually subject to appellate review. Judges decide matters of law, not value-laden policy questions. Judges must substantiate their legal conclusions by issuing a written opinion. And judges in all 50 states are governed by an ethical code, in writing, with prescribed remedies and enforcement procedures.

Among their ethical prohibitions, judges may not hear cases in which they have a personal bias toward a party or a financial interest in a party or in the subject matter. Moreover, the ABA Model Code of Judicial Conduct, adopted in substance by 47 states, permits fundraising only by "committees of responsible persons" acting on behalf of the nominee. Candidates may not directly solicit or accept campaign contributions. In August 1999, the ABA went considerably further. It modified the Model Code to command that judges disqualify themselves from any case in which a party or attorney has donated more than a specified amount (to be determined by each state). That anti-corruption provision is buttressed by comprehensive disclosure obligations.

Unquestionably, the requirement that judges recuse themselves in appropriate cases is less restrictive medicine than compelled speech. Indeed, even the ABA's disclosure mandate can be avoided if parties and attorneys simply declare under penalty of perjury that they have not violated established contribution limits. That way, both political coercion and influence peddling are minimized. At the same time, voters will be free to advance their particular judicial philosophies by contributing to the campaign of their choice.

Contested judicial elections may be a bad idea, but without free speech they are immeasurably worse.

Periodical Bibliography

The following articles have been selected to supplement the diverse views presented in this chapter.

Lawton "Bud" Chiles	"Fair Elections Now Act Needs Support," *Sun Sentinel*, November 14, 2010.
Sattie Clark and Mike Roach	"Voter-Owned Elections Have Shown Their Value," *Portland Tribune*, September 30, 2010.
Stephen Dinan	"House Votes for Repeal of Public-Paid Campaigns," *Washington Times*, January 26, 2011.
Murray Galinson	"Congress Must Address Broken Political System," *Sign On San Diego*, November 26, 2010.
Simon Lee	"Public Financing Is Only Way to Stop Absurd Campaign Costs," Bakersfield.com, November 2, 2010.
Susan Linn and Monica Youn	"Fair Elections: A Constitutional Safe Harbor," Brennan Center for Justice, September 15, 2010.
Don McGahn	"End Federal Handouts to Political Campaigns," *Washington Examiner*, January 24, 2011.
Alyssa Newcomb	"What Clean Elections Money Bought," azcentral.com, November 28, 2010.
Bruce Ramsey	"Kill Campaign-Finance Reform with the First Amendment," *Seattle Times*, December 7, 2010.
Brad Smith	"Fair Elections Now: When Life Gives You Lemons, Pretend Reality Doesn't Exist," Center for Competitive Politics, November 6, 2010.
Daniel Weeks	"Empower the American People, Not Special Interests, to Bankroll Elections," Progressive Policy Institute, September 22, 2010.

OPPOSING
VIEWPOINTS®
SERIES

CHAPTER 3

Does Campaign Finance Reform Effectively Regulate Election Spending?

Chapter Preface

The creation of the Federal Election Commission (FEC) was mandated as part of the 1975 amendment to update the Federal Election Campaign Act (FECA) of 1971. It also was a response to revelations that emerged from hearings convened by the US Senate Watergate Committee from May 1973 to June 1974 that implicated then-president Richard Nixon in one of the most notorious political scandals in US history and also exposed the depths of corruption in the American campaign fundraising system.

Even as a candidate in the election to represent his California district in the House of Representatives in 1950, Nixon had shown himself willing to accept money from anyone who wanted to contribute, including Mafia members, in exchange for political favors. In 1969, Nixon was elected president, and in preparation for the upcoming mid-term elections, he directed his White House chief of staff, H.R. Haldeman, to create a secret campaign fund to collect contributions from wealthy businessmen in order to funnel the money to the campaigns of politicians Nixon considered loyal to him. Donors at the time included technology entrepreneur H. Ross Perot, Hollywood producer-director Howard Hughes, and the president of PepsiCo, among others. One of the politicians who benefited most from Nixon's secret fund was future president George H.W. Bush, although he lost his 1970 bid for a Senate seat. In 1971, Nixon courted the endorsement of and donations from Associated Milk Producers, Inc. (AMPI), a large cooperative of US milk producers, by promising to drive up milk prices artificially if the group agreed to contribute funds to his reelection campaign.

In 1972, the Nixon administration created the Campaign to Re-elect the President (CRP, also known as CREEP), which routinely paid out money to individuals from its campaign fund. One of the largest donors to the CRP was the company ITT, which was at the time involved in an antitrust lawsuit. Nixon promised to intervene in the suit in exchange for more cash donations, and the lawsuit against ITT was dismissed by the US Department of Justice in July 1971. In the meantime, two *Washington Post* reporters, Carl Bernstein and Bob Woodward, began to investigate the story of a break-in at the headquarters of the Democratic National Committee (DNC) at the Watergate Hotel in Washington, D.C., including allegations that members of Nixon's circle were involved in the break-in.

In June 1972, five men with ties to the CRP were arrested inside DNC offices; eventually it was discovered that most of those involved had received cash payments from the CRP funds. Federal Bureau of Investigation (FBI) agents found in September 1972 that Nixon's attorney general, John Mitchell, was personally in charge of dispensing funds to spy on the DNC. The following month the full extent of the connections between the Watergate affair, as it had become known, and the Nixon administration were made public.

The Federal Election Campaign Act had passed in early 1971, but it did not go into effect until April of that year. In anticipation of FECA, Nixon sent out orders to CRP members to collect as much money as possible before April to avoid having to report the funds under the terms of the new campaign finance legislation. Nixon promised ambassadorships to donors of at least $250,000. CRP collected a total of $20 million, much of which was laundered through banks in Mexico and Venezuela. Money donated directly by corporations—who were at the time banned from contributing to federal election campaigns—also was laundered through Mexican banks.

Nixon was elected to a second term in November 1972 despite questions about his involvement in the increasingly complex scandal. But as more and more members of his administration and the CRP were found to have been involved, Nixon himself was implicated. In April 1973, Nixon's vice president

Spiro Agnew was accused of accepting illegal campaign contributions in his home state of Maryland. Further investigation of the CRP proved that much of the money collected from donors was used illegally. Finally, in March 1974, seven members of the administration were indicted for Watergate crimes by a federal grand jury. Nixon avoided indictment and was named an "unindicted co-conspirator" in the scandal. In March 1974, Nixon resigned from office, having headed what was widely considered the most corrupt presidential administration in US history.

The viewpoints in the following chapter discuss the role of campaign finance reform in election spending. The authors touch on the effects of the Democracy Is Strengthened by Casting Light on Spending in Elections (DISCLOSE) Act, the Federal Election Commission, and the impact of the *Citizens United v. Federal Election Commission* Supreme Court decision on campaign finance reform.

> *"The Supreme Court sort of dumped on all of us this new Wild Wild West approach in campaign finance, unlimited corporation and union spending for independent messaging . . . , and that . . . to most of us doesn't seem like a healthy political system."*

The DISCLOSE Act Is Necessary to Enforce Campaign Finance Reform

Chris Good

Chris Good is an associate editor at the Atlantic. *Trevor Potter and Scott Thomas are both former heads of the Federal Election Commission. In the following viewpoint, Good highlights Potter and Thomas's strenuous arguments in favor of rapid implementation of the Democracy Is Strengthened by Casting Light on Spending in Elections (DISCLOSE) Act. Both maintain that the DISCLOSE Act is greatly needed following the* Citizens United v. Federal Election Commission *Supreme Court decision and that disclosure regulations were clearly ruled constitutional as part of this same decision.*

As you read, consider the following questions:

1. What does Trevor Potter cite as the Supreme Court's view in *Citizens United* on mandated disclosure of contributors?

2. What does Trevor Potter mean by "partisan deadlock in Congress" over the issue of disclosure?

3. According to Scott Thomas, what would the Federal Election Commission have to do to implement quickly the DISCLOSE Act if it were to pass through Congress?

Several groups that support the DISCLOSE [Democracy Is Strengthened by Casting Light on Spending in Elections] Act, the Democratic campaign finance reform bill that is being pushed as a response to the Supreme Court's *Citizens United* decision, organized a conference call with reporters today on which two former chairman of the Federal Election Commission [FEC] spoke out in favor of the bill.

The legislation seeks to impose stricter disclosure requirements on corporate spending. Under current FEC regulation, corporations are already required to disclose their independent campaign spending (e.g., to run ads separate from donations to candidates), but the DISCLOSE Act requires CEOs [chief executive officers], for instance, to make statements at the end of ads and disclose where the funding for the ad came from. Here's what they had to say on the call, hosted by the League of Women Voters of Maine, U.S. PIRG [Federation of State Public Interest Research Groups], the Campaign Legal Center, Public Citizen, and Democracy 21.

Citizens and Shareholders Should Know How Their Money Is Spent

Trevor Potter, a former counsel for [former President] George H.W. Bush who chaired the Federal Election Commission from 1991–1995, is founding president of the Campaign Legal

The Truth About the DISCLOSE Act

Myth: The DISCLOSE [Democracy Is Strengthened by Casting Light on Spending in Elections] Act is designed to benefit Democrats and labor unions and disadvantage Republicans and corporations.

Reality: The DISCLOSE Act is designed to benefit the American people by providing them with essential campaign finance information about unions and corporations spending money to influence the election of Democratic and Republican federal candidates. Opponents of this legislation would deny voters campaign finance information they have a fundamental right to know, as affirmed by the Supreme Court in the *Citizens United* decision.

Fred Wertheimer,
"Myths and Realities Regarding Claims that Labor Unions
Are Treated More Favorably Than Corporations By the
DISCLOSE Act Passed in June by the House and Pending
in the Senate," Democracy21.com, July 19, 2010.

Center and an attorney for Caplin & Drysdale. He said:

The pressure that we're under, as a country, is that the Supreme Court's *Citizens United* decision announced last winter was effective immediately, so it covers all spending in this election year, and there have been people, Sen. [Scott] Brown of Massachusetts recently, that he said he thought it was too much of a rush to try to do something to cover this election. Unfortunately the Supreme Court didn't really leave us a choice, because they covered this election in their decision for the first time in history allowing corporations and unions to spend unlimited funds in federal elections, so the point of the DISCLOSE Act is to know who is doing that spending, and current law has some significant holes in the disclosure fabric.

It is possible, as I think all of us are aware, to run ads that say something like, 'Paid for by Americans for a Better Country.' You have no idea who that is or who actually paid for those ads, even if you have a well known group like the Chamber of Commerce, so it says, 'Paid for by the Maine Chamber of Commerce,' they don't report publicly who their donors are or who specifically provided money that they're using for this ad, so that it is possible to have a lot of spending in elections with a vague or no idea of where that spending is coming from. The Supreme Court in the *Citizens United* case, interestingly, made it absolutely clear, there was an 8-1 vote, on the proposition that all of this election advertising can be disclosed—that the government may require the disclosure of the sources of funding in these ads, and Justice [Anthony M.] Kennedy, who had written the majority opinion saying corporations could spend this money and unions, specifically said that there was a real interest in not just citizens but also shareholders knowing how their money was being spent, and that such disclosure requirements were constitutionally permissible.

So we have a case here where we have a real urgent need, we have a Supreme Court decision that said as clearly as it could that it is constitutional to require such disclosure, and we have a partisan deadlock in Congress, the Republicans pretty much uniformly having decided that they would rather not have this sort of disclosure this year. As a Republican, obviously, that pains me, particularly because for years the opponents of campaign finance reform said, well all we needed was disclosure, and now that that's all we're going to get, they don't want us to have that either. So I have been urging Republicans to step forward. I know there are questions about portions of the bill, and the House bill is not perfect—no single piece of legislation ever is perfect—but what I'm hoping is that Republican senators who have long stood for reform will reach across the aisle and figure out with the Democratic leadership what needs to be done to make this a bill that they and ideally other Republicans can support.

The Supreme Court Decision Is New Territory

Scott Thomas, a former staff attorney at the Federal Election Commission, served three terms as Federal Election Commission chairman from 1986–2006 and is now an attorney for Dickstein Shapiro. He said:

> I think I can safely address the arguments about whether or not there should be some sort of slowdown in passage of this legislation or halting because it might be better if the FEC had a lot of time to implement this with regulations, and if the FEC were able to go through its normal process for putting up for comment draft regulations to implement the law. And my sense of it is, as Trevor Potter noted, this is a very special, unique set of circumstances. The Supreme Court sort of dumped on all of us this new Wild Wild West approach in campaign finance, unlimited corporation and union spending for independent messaging, and we just are in a position where there may be huge amounts of money spent and just totally inadequate disclosure about who's actually behind this, and that, just, to most of us doesn't seem like a healthy political system.

> But I would say the Federal Election Commission would be obviously under some pressure to try to move quickly on those things it does have to do, but the reality is they don't really have to do anything that would be highly controversial at all. They would want to obviously implement some new forms to facilitate the new disclosure standards that are being set up for these independent expenditures and electioneering communications, but those substantive provisions are all very clearly laid out in the statutory changes. The level of detail is [all] there in the DISCLOSE Act. There wouldn't really be a need to add any sort of substantive interpretations, at least in the short term, and so I'm quite confident the commission could adopt some forms that would help with the disclosure implementation, and as to the other parts of the law that change some of the contribu-

tion restrictions for domestic subsidiaries of foreign corporations and so on, or that impose some new disclaimer requirements, again those standards are all very clearly built
into this legislation. It's been carefully crafted to be precise
and clear enough on its own, and so I'm confident the FEC
could quickly get out the message to everybody that's out
there in the regulated community, and it would be a kind of
a piece of legislation that could basically start in operation
right away, and I don't think there's really a need for holding things up simply on that kind of a concern.

> "*The real effects of the DISCLOSE Act will be to deter political speech . . . and political advocacy by corporations and associations that Democrats don't want participating in the American political process.*"

The DISCLOSE Act Is Unconstitutional and Unfairly Burdens Corporations

Hans A. von Spakovsky

Hans A. von Spakovsky manages the Civil Justice Reform Initiative at the Heritage Foundation's Center for Legal and Judicial Studies, where he is a senior legal fellow. In the following viewpoint, von Spakovsky argues that the Democracy Is Strengthened by Casting Light on Spending in Elections (DISCLOSE) Act is a thoroughly partisan piece of legislation designed to make political speech as difficult as possible and eliminate any outside influence from government. The author also claims that requiring donor disclosure violates corporations' First Amendment right to free speech by subjecting them to regulations that are not placed on nonprofit organizations.

Hans A. von Spakovsky, "Obama Klan's Attempt at a Modern-Day Alien and Sedition Acts: The DISCLOSE Act," *Capitalism Magazine*, June 25, 2010. Copyright © 2010 by The Heritage Foundation. Reproduced by permission.

As you read, consider the following questions:

1. Who are the congressional sponsors of the DISCLOSE Act?

2. According to the author, who was the target of the 1798 Alien and Sedition Acts?

3. Which organization does the author accuse of betraying the cause of free speech?

You'd think that members of Congress would have a keen knowledge of and appreciation for congressional history; you'd think they would know better than to repeat the mistakes made by their legislative body in the past. But if partisanship guides your actions and winning elections at all costs is your objective, then repeating unconstitutional behavior is apparently not beyond the pale.

That is exactly what is about to happen: The House of Representatives is expected to vote in the next day or two [June 2010] on the DISCLOSE (Democracy Is Strengthened by Casting Light on Spending in Elections) Act, a law purportedly intended to blunt the effects of the Supreme Court's *Citizens United v. FEC* [Federal Election Commission] decision. That case restored the First Amendment right of political speech by throwing out a federal ban on independent political advocacy by unions and corporations, including both for-profit and non-profit associations.

The real effects of the DISCLOSE Act will be to deter political speech (including criticism of incumbents, such as its chief sponsors, Sen. Chuck Schumer (D-NY) and Rep. Chris Van Hollen (D-MD)) and political advocacy by corporations and associations that Democrats don't want participating in the American political process. It includes both absolute bans on independent political advocacy and new, burdensome disclosure requirements. Schumer admitted when he introduced the bill that "the deterrent effect should not be underestimated." During a House Administration Committee hearing, Rep. Michael Capuano (D-MA) made no bones about the fact that he hoped this Act "chills out all . . . I have no problem whatsoever keeping everybody out [of elections]. If I could keep all outside entities out, I would."

Of course, the "deterrent" and "chilling" effect is meant to hit corporations—including nonprofit associations like Citizens United, the conservative advocacy organization that brought the original lawsuit—but not unions, which are exempted from most of the provisions of the bill. No surprise there, since unions support Democrats almost exclusively, with huge amounts of money. And the majority party is moving this bill at a breakneck pace through Congress to have it in place for the November elections, because Democrats fear November will be their election Waterloo.

Modern-Day Federalist-Type Censorship

The DISCLOSE Act would ban certain government contractors from engaging in any political speech, yet unions that represent government employees, and organizations like Planned Parenthood that receive large amounts of federal grants, would not be affected. American companies with American workers and American officers could be banned from speaking if a small minority of their shareholders are foreigners, yet unions with foreign officers and foreign members could spend as much money on political advocacy as they want. And many of the new disclosure provisions imposed by the act were made onerous and burdensome for the specific purpose of deterring political speech.

If all of this sounds depressingly familiar, it should. The DISCLOSE Act is the modern-day version of the Alien and Sedition Acts, which were passed by the Federalists in 1798 to quell political opposition from the Republicans, led by Thomas Jefferson. These acts were one of the worst (and most noxious) violations of the First Amendment ever passed by

Congress. Under their terms, Federalist judges jailed or fined 25 people, mostly Republican newspaper editors, and many of their newspapers were forced to shut down.

One of the men arrested was Benjamin Franklin's grandson, Benjamin Franklin Bache. Another was Rep. Matthew Lyon, who was jailed while a Republican congressman from Vermont and won reelection behind bars. The first man arrested was Luther Baldwin, of New Jersey, who was convicted and fined $100 for wishing that a blast from the presidential saluting-cannon would hit Pres. John Adams in "his arse." Under the DISCLOSE Act, if a corporate association met the qualifications for the government-contractor ban on independent expenditures and ran an ad saying the same thing about President [Barack] Obama in 2012, it could also be fined and its corporate officers sent to jail.

Traitors of the Cause

As always, there are those willing to sacrifice liberty in order to gain a personal or political advantage for themselves. The National Rifle Association [NRA], which previously called the *Citizens United* decision a "defeat for arrogant elitists who wanted to carve out free speech as a privilege for themselves and deny it to the rest of us," has apparently agreed to withdraw its opposition to the DISCLOSE Act in exchange for a narrowly drawn exemption. Instead of applying to all nonprofit advocacy groups, including the smaller, less powerful ones with limited budgets that will be particularly affected and burdened by these new regulations, the exemption will apply only to 501(c)(4) organizations with members in all 50 states, numbering more than one million overall, that have been in existence for ten years and receive 15 percent or less of their funds from corporations. The NRA, a well-funded, powerful organization, coincidentally fits within this exemption. So the NRA has received its 30 pieces of silver in return for forsaking the political speech rights of the rest of us.

Public opposition to the Alien and Sedition Acts was so great that it was major factor in the election of Thomas Jefferson as president in 1800. Although Adams neither vetoed nor protested these Acts, he was apparently embarrassed enough about their passage that he later denied any responsibility for them. Unfortunately, neither the members of Congress pushing the DISCLOSE Act nor the president seem at all embarrassed about this pending abrogation of basic First Amendment free-speech and associational rights. If the unconstitutional, partisan, and pernicious DISCLOSE Act is passed and signed into law by President Obama, it will be interesting to see if the American public has same reaction to this noxious bill in 2010 and 2012 that the public had in 1800.

> *"Blame for the current drop off in disclosure falls not at the feet of the Supreme Court, but at the feet of the FEC [Federal Election Commission], an agency so mired in gridlock that it is part unable and part unwilling to enforce its own guiding statutes."*

The Federal Election Commission Hinders Campaign Finance Reform

Jesse Zwick

Jesse Zwick is a writer and researcher at the New Republic. *In the following viewpoint, Zwick maintains that any election funding legislation will be pointless because the Federal Election Commission (FEC) is itself systemically incapable of and unwilling to enforce any laws. Zwick points out that, as of late 2010, three of the six commissioners who head the FEC were serving beyond their terms, and replacing them did not appear to be a priority for the administration of President Barack Obama because it would likely bring on a political battle with congressional Republicans. The way the FEC is designed, according to*

Zwick, runs counter to successful functioning as well, with the mandate that it be evenly divided according to political partisanship.

As you read, consider the following questions:

1. According to the author, what is the main problem with the way the FEC was designed?

2. According to the viewpoint, what is FEC Commissioner Donald McGahn's view of the FEC?

3. From which members of the Senate must the president seek suggestions for new FEC commissioners, according to the viewpoint?

Campaign finance reform groups are telling a sobering story. During the 2004 and 2006 elections, nonprofit groups reported who donated nearly every penny spent on independent advertisements mentioning candidates (called electioneering communications) to the Federal Election Commission [FEC]. In 2008, they accounted for less than two-thirds of the dollars behind the ads. And in the current primary season, reporting has fallen by about one-half again. Just one-third of the dollars spent on such ads were tracked back to their donors.

The precipitous decline comes in the wake of the Supreme Court's decision in *Citizens United v. Federal Election Commission*. The January 2010 ruling allowed corporations or labor unions to spend unlimited sums of money to advocate on behalf of candidates; previously, only individuals or groups of individuals could do so. And many well-meaning citizens and politicians blame the rise in opacity on the ruling.

But the falloff in disclosure started long before the Court's decision. And blame for the current drop off in disclosure falls not at the feet of the Supreme Court, but at the feet of the FEC, an agency so mired in gridlock that it is part unable and part unwilling to enforce its own guiding statutes.

"It's essential to put the national spotlight on the FEC," notes Fred Wertheimer, president of Democracy 21, an organization that advocates for campaign finance reform in Congress and in the courts. "I do not think that most citizens know that, for all practical purposes, we do not have a campaign finance enforcement agency. We have a set of laws on the books, but we have an agency that basically refuses to enforce them, or misinterprets the laws in ways that cripples their impact."

Congress is trying (and, thus far, failing) to strengthen campaign finance and disclosure laws, with legislation like the DISCLOSE [Democracy Is Strengthened by Casting Light on Spending in Elections] Act. But reformers argue that legislation is not the only way to shore up donor disclosure. The FEC currently lacks the willpower, but not the prerogative, to enforce disclosure laws that exist on the books, and three of its six current commissioners are serving past the end of their designated terms. The [President Barack] Obama administration, advocates note, could appoint new, committed commissioners to take their seats, but thus far it has shied away from the political fight with Republican leadership that would be required to make it happen.

A Commission Divided

As a body, the FEC has never been mistaken for a paragon of nonpartisan professionalism, or even mere efficiency—and a portion of that has to do with the way it was set up. Designed so that no political party is allowed to claim the allegiance of more than three of its six serving commissioners, any action taken by the commission necessarily requires at least one commissioner to cross the political aisle.

"[Those who designed it] either knew they were intentionally creating a dysfunctional agency or they were not familiar with decision-making processes and how it might work out," says Paul Ryan, associate legal counsel at the Campaign Legal

Center. "The agency was designed to deadlock," he adds, and "if you look at it from perspective of members of Congress creating an agency tasked with policing them, we too might choose to create a less-than-functional agency."

Yet despite its partisan design, for much of its history the commission rarely deadlocked, especially when it came to decisions regarding enforcement proceedings against political groups believed to have broken campaign-finance laws.

A recent report from Public Citizen, a nonprofit consumer advocacy organization, argues the real trouble started in mid-2008, when Congress confirmed three new Republican commissioners—Caroline Hunter, Donald McGahn, and Matthew Petersen—to the regulatory body. The proportion of enforcement actions stalled in the FEC at that point jumped from less than 2 percent per year to 16 percent in 2009. In 2010, "all I can think of are deadlocked votes," says the report's author, Public Citizen's legislative representative Craig Holman.

An Ideological FEC

While commissioners had always displayed flashes of partisan politics, the new GOP [Republican] members went a step beyond, displaying an ideological mistrust of any effort to enforce regulations that might deter the political speech of political groups supporting either party—regulations that they, as commissioners, were tasked with the duty of enforcing.

"These three individuals on the commission have made it very clear that they are ideologically opposed to campaign finance laws and prepared to take extreme steps to make sure that they have minimal impact and make sure that they are not enforced," Wertheimer says.

Commissioner Donald McGahn, in particular, is often cited as the ringleader of the current GOP voting bloc and the architect of its disciplined comment to block all critical enforcement matters. McGahn served as a campaign finance and ethics lawyer for former House Majority Leader Tom DeLay, whose violations of campaign finance laws made his name synonymous with Beltway corruption. McGahn also rigidly opposes the idea of campaign finance regulation itself. He "views enforcement of the law as an infringement of rights," argues Ryan, "and has often expressed a fair degree of hostility to the very purpose of the commission itself."

True to their sentiments, four times in 2008 the GOP commissioners rebuffed the FEC's own staff lawyers' recommendations to investigate different groups believed to have skirted the body's regulations. And on a 3-3 party-line vote, the GOP commissioners even refused to accept a punitive fine that the FEC counsel had previously negotiated with a U.S. Chamber of Commerce-funded group for improprieties committed in a previous election cycle.

Donor Disclosure Begone

The final nail in the coffin of donor disclosure, however, came earlier this year when the FEC declined in a party-line vote to pursue an investigation into the now-defunct organization, Freedom's Watch, effectively absolving the group for failing to report any donors for the vast majority of its electioneering communications in 2008.

Both the DCCC [Democratic Congressional Campaign Committee], which originally filed the complaint and the FEC's own staff, which recommended an investigation, had cited a *New York Times* article that quoted anonymous Republican operatives and reported that the group's approximately $30 million for ad spending "came almost entirely from casino mogul Sheldon Adelson, who has 'insisted on parceling out his money project-by-project.'" In their justification for not taking action, however, the Republican commissioners ridiculed the *Times'* use of anonymous sources and, more importantly, substantially reinterpreted and narrowed the FEC regulations outlining the conditions in which donor disclosure must take place.

While current regulations dictate that all donations of more than $1,000 made "for the purpose of furthering electioneering communications" must be disclosed to the FEC, the GOP commissioners argued that since the $126,000 ad in question could, in theory, have been funded by other donors besides Adelson, the group was under no obligation to report their primary backer's involvement in the ad. In other words, the GOP commissioners now argued that unless a specific donor contribution could be demonstrably linked to the creation of a specific ad—a practice no political donors engage in—nonprofit groups that cut political ads were under no requirement to disclose their donor rolls.

"[The GOP commissioners] locked down on the interpretation that there must be some sort of written or oral designation by the contributor that the money is going to a specific ad at a specific time in a specific place, and nobody does that," explains Holman. "As a result they've shut down all disclosure."

The impact of the FEC's decision, meanwhile, has extended far beyond the individual enforcement case at hand. Rather, it has contributed to what Wertheimer describes as a "Wild West situation where there's nothing to worry about as far as complying with campaign finance laws." 501(c) [nonprofit] organizations—the group of choice for influencing political races in the current election cycle—now feel little fear of reprisal when they list ".00" on their electioneering communication reports under the area for donor contributions, and the ever increasing number of groups abstaining from the practice of disclosure attests to their sense of impunity.

No Appetite for Reform

Fixing the FEC by reforming its basic, gridlocked structure would require new legislation that's simply out of the question at this point, reform advocates argue. But naming new appointees to replace the three commissioners—including

The FEC Is Ineffective and Should Be Replaced

The record of FEC [Federal Election Commission] failure is as long as the agency's history, and it continues. . . .

Congress gave the FEC few actual powers compared to other law enforcement agencies. The FEC cannot sanction groups it believes have violated the law—it can only negotiate for a payment of civil penalties. If it cannot reach a settlement, the FEC can then begin an enforcement action in court by filing a civil lawsuit. The commission cannot seek court injunctions to halt illegal activity nor can it conduct random audits of campaigns.

The FEC is not a credible deterrent to illegal campaign activities, even when it is functioning. It is time to rethink how we enforce our campaign finance laws. Common Cause calls for:

1. A new independent Federal Election Administration, as outlined in the pending McCain/Meehan bills (S. 478 and H.R. 421) introduced in the 110th Congress, with enforcement proceedings conducted by Administrative Law Judges.

2. In the meantime, the [Barack] Obama Administration should convene a blue ribbon panel to pick highly qualified, independent nominees to fill the three vacant FEC posts expected to occur in spring 2009. . . .

The strict partisanship of the appointment process for the FEC has helped to ensure that it remains deadlocked, resulting in a collapse of enforcement—and just as importantly—the belief that the rules are unlikely to be enforced, which encourages donors and campaigns to try to skirt or violate the law.

"Campaign Finance Reform: A New Era,"
Commoncause.org, January 2009.

McGahn—whose terms have long since expired is doable. But even though McGahn, along with Democratic commissioners Ellen Weintraub and Steven Walther, are all serving in a lame-duck capacity, the Obama administration has made hardly any effort to replace them.

The reason for Obama's inaction, advocates speculate, is that custom dictates that the President ask the Majority and Minority Leaders of the Senate to submit names for the FEC commissioner positions and nominate them accordingly. But Minority Leader Sen. Mitch McConnell (R-Ky.), who has vociferously opposed the DISCLOSE Act in the Senate, is hardly motivated to disrupt the body's current gridlock and even more unlikely to recommend a commissioner whose beliefs would stray from his own, rigid distaste for campaign finance regulation.

"Where the commission has broken down is with the appointment process to the FEC," notes Holman. "Even though legally the process is that the president appoints commissioners with the confirmation and advice of Senate, it's really always been the other way around . . . and McConnell started realizing some time ago that he could wreck havoc through the appointment process."

The administration, in other words, is free to nominate a Republican or an independent appointee to replace McGahn tomorrow. But doing so would be sure to ruffle some feathers.

"[Obama] could nominate new commissioners and send them up to the Senate," notes Wertheimer, "and if McConnell used his influence to filibuster or block the appointments, then he could consider recess appointments. To date it's simply been not important enough in their minds to take on McConnell."

The Administration Is Slow to Move

Indeed, the only action the administration has attempted since taking office was in 2009 when it appointed Democratic union lawyer John Sullivan to replace one of the Democratic commissioners, a move that Sens. John McCain (R-Ariz.) and Russ Feingold (D-Wis.) announced they would block until the president agreed to submit nominations to replace all three lame duck commissioners at once.

McCain and Feingold, who co-sponsored the Bipartisan Campaign Reform Act in 2002 and have been frustrated with the FEC's refusal to adequately enforce the bill's statutes, released a statement at the time that urged the president to "nominate new commissioners with a demonstrated commitment to the existence and enforcement of the campaign finance laws," but since then the administration has been mum. (Probed about the ongoing delay in nominating new FEC commissioners, a White House spokesman could only say "the President is committed to filling these positions with the most qualified persons.")

Reform advocates, while eager to get the commissioners replaced, nonetheless sided with the two senators, in part because Obama's pick hardly represented the kind of integrity and commitment to campaign finance laws for which they were hoping. "My concern with Sullivan's nomination is that he has made a career out of fighting FEC regulations for labor unions," Ryan says. "It didn't represent one iota of change."

> *"Alarmists say the court's ruling will mean torrential spending by large for-profit corporations. . . . Wrong. Corporate contributions to candidates' campaigns remain proscribed."*

The Federal Election Commission Already Successfully Monitors Election Spending

George F. Will

George F. Will is a writer and political commentator who contributes columns to the Washington Post *and other newspapers. In the following viewpoint, Will argues that the* Citizens United v. Federal Election Commission *court decision was the proper response to a system overburdened by regulations. Will also asserts that the Federal Election Commission's oversight of and authority over corporate campaign contributions remains intact following the* Citizens United *ruling, and he says fears of corporate takeovers are unfounded. Additionally, Will contends that mandating strict regulation of political speech—including finan-*

cial campaign contributions—downplays the ability of voters to judge for themselves what they see and hear in political advertisements and publications.

As you read, consider the following questions:

1. How many kinds of political speech have been identified by the Federal Election Commission, according to Will?

2. Which groups, according to finance attorney Cleta Mitchell, will benefit most from the *Citizens United* decision?

3. According to the author, what is the public's apparent position on publicly financed elections?

Last week's [January 2010] Supreme Court decision that substantially deregulates political speech has provoked an edifying torrent of hyperbole. Critics' dismay reveals their conviction: Speech about the elections that determine the government's composition is not a constitutional right but a mere privilege that exists at the sufferance of government.

How regulated did political speech become during the decades when the court was derelict in its duty to actively defend the Constitution? The Federal Election Commission [FEC], which administers the law that rations the quantity and regulates the content and timing of political speech, identifies 33 types of political speech and 71 kinds of "speakers." The underlying statute and FEC regulations cover more than 800 pages, and FEC explanations of its decisions have filled more than 1,200 pages. The First Amendment requires 10 words for a sufficient stipulation: "Congress shall make no law ... abridging the freedom of speech."

Extending the logic of a 1976 decision, the court has now held that the dissemination of political speech requires money, so restricting money restricts speech. Bringing law into conformity with this 1976 precedent, the court has struck down only federal and state laws that forbid *independent* expenditures (those not made directly to, or coordinated with, candidates' campaigns) by corporations *and labor unions*. Under the censorship regime the court has overturned, corporations were even forbidden to send political communications to all of their employees.

The Alarmist Response

The *New York Times* calls the court's decision, which enables political advocacy by (other) corporations, a "blow to democracy." The *Times*, a corporate entity, can engage in political advocacy because Congress has granted "media corporations" an exemption from limits.

The *Washington Post*, also exempt, says the court's decision, which overturned a previous ruling upholding restrictions on spending for political speech, shows insufficient "respect for precedent." Does The *Post* think the court incorrectly overturned precedents that upheld racial segregation and warrantless wiretaps? Are the only sacrosanct precedents those that abridge (others') right to speak?

Alarmists say the court's ruling will mean torrential spending by large for-profit corporations. Anna Burger, secretary-treasurer of the Service Employees International Union—it has spent $20 million on politics in the past five election cycles—says a corporation will "funnel their shareholders' money straight to a campaign's coffers." Wrong. Corporate contributions to candidates' campaigns remain proscribed.

Cleta Mitchell, Washington's preeminent campaign finance attorney, rightly says that few for-profit corporations will jeopardize their commercial interests by engaging in partisan politics: Republicans, Democrats and independents buy Microsoft's and Pepsi's products. If for-profit corporations do plunge into politics, disclosure of their spending will enable voters to draw appropriate conclusions. Of course, political speech regulations radiate distrust of voters' abilities to assess unfettered political advocacy.

Mitchell says the court's decision primarily liberates non-profit advocacy groups, such as the Sierra Club, which the FEC fined $28,000 in 2006. The club's sin was to distribute pamphlet's in Florida contrasting the environmental views of the presidential and senatorial candidates, to the intended advantage of Democrats. FEC censors deemed this an illegal corporate contribution.

Public Financing Is "Wildly Unpopular"

[President] Barack "Pitchfork" Obama, in his post-Massachusetts populist mode, called the court's ruling a victory for, among others, "big oil" and "Wall Street banks." But OpenSecrets.org reports that in 2008 lawyers gave more money than either of them, and gave 78 percent of the donations to Democrats, who also received 64 percent of contributions from the financial sector.

Even if it were Congress's business to decide that there is "too much" money in politics, that decision would be odd: In the 2007–08 election cycle, spending in all campaigns, for city council members up to the presidency, was $8.6 billion, about what Americans spend *annually* on potato chips.

Critics say raising such sums requires too much of candidates' time. Well, then, let candidates receive unlimited—but fully disclosed—contributions, and trust voters to make appropriate inferences about the candidates.

Undaunted, advocates of government control of political speech want Congress to enact public financing of congressional campaigns, and to ban individuals from participating in politics through contributions. Fortunately, this idea—"food stamps for politicians"—is wildly unpopular. Public financing of presidential campaigns has collapsed. Obama disdained it in 2008; the public always has. Voluntary, cost-free participation, using the checkoff on the income tax form, peaked at a paltry 28.7 percent in 1980 and by 2008 had sagged to 8.3 percent.

This is redundant proof that the premise of campaign finance "reform" is false. The premise is that easily befuddled Americans need to be swaddled in regulations of political speech.

> "The attention drawn by the Citizens United decision has obscured the many additional challenges to existing campaign finance laws ... that are making their way through the lower courts in the hope of finding a sympathetic audience before the Supreme Court."

The *Citizens United* Decision Destroys Meaningful Campaign Finance Reform

J. Gerald Hebert and Tara Malloy

J. Gerald Hebert is executive director and director of litigation for the Campaign Legal Center. Tara Malloy is associate legal counsel at the Campaign Legal Center. In the following viewpoint, the authors trace the litigation brought against numerous pieces of campaign finance reform legislation since the Citizens United *ruling, a landmark decision in 2010 by the US Supreme Court holding that corporate funding of independent political broadcasts in candidate elections cannot be limited. The authors maintain that the decision has resulted in a generally combative*

J. Gerald Hebert and Tara Malloy, "Challenges to Campaign Finance and Disclosure Laws Multiply after *Citizens United* Ruling from Roberts Court," *Campaign Legal Center Blog*, May 21, 2010. Copyright © 2010 by Campaign Legal Center. Reproduced by permission.

mood among anti-reform groups. Referring to a "long-term litigation offensive," Hebert and Malloy contend that efforts at campaign finance reform are being stymied by a campaign of lawsuits brought by anti-reform groups to clog the court system and slow the campaign reform effort.

As you read, consider the following questions:

1. According to the viewpoint, which two organizations are behind the majority of the litigation against campaign finance reform legislation?

2. How many cases in federal and state courts has the Campaign Legal Center counted since 2007?

3. What do the authors maintain is the ultimate purpose of legal challenges to campaign finance laws?

In January 2010, the [US Supreme Court Justice John] Roberts Court in *Citizens United v. FEC* [Federal Election Commission] abandoned any pretense of its claimed commitment to judicial modesty and respect for precedent, and overruled two seminal campaign finance cases: *Austin v. Michigan Chamber of Commerce* and *McConnell v. FEC.*

The *Citizens United* decision effectively authorized corporations and unions to make unlimited expenditures of treasury funds to influence federal and state elections. This radical step captured the nation's attention, drawing widespread public outrage, the ire of the White House, and a legislative response from Congress aiming to mitigate the damage inflicted by the ruling.

Other Challenges to Campaign Finance Laws

However, the attention drawn by the *Citizens United* decision has obscured the many additional challenges to existing campaign finance laws—including challenges to simple donor disclosure requirements—that are making their way through the lower courts in the hope of finding a sympathetic audience before the Supreme Court.

These challenges are a part of a systematic, long-term litigation offensive mounted by deep-pocketed interests who are opposed to any type of regulation of political spending. Emboldened by the conservative majority in the U.S. Supreme Court, national party committees, trade associations, ideological groups, so-called "527" organizations and other opponents of campaign finance regulation have brought an unprecedented number of cases in the past three years to challenge campaign finance laws at the federal, state and municipal levels. *Citizens United* may constitute their greatest success thus far, but the decision is by no means the endpoint of their efforts. Instead, as their counsel have openly conceded, this anti-reform effort aims to dismantle contribution limits, public finance programs, the remaining limitations on corporate and union political activity and most accompanying disclosure requirements.

Litigators Launch Attacks

A great number of the challenges in recent years have been filed by two well funded organizations that reveal little to nothing about the sources of their funding: The James Madison Center for Free Speech and the Center for Competitive Politics (CCP).

The Madison Center is headed up by James Bopp, Jr., an RNC [Republican National Committee] Committeeman and the attorney who launched the initial *Citizens United* challenge to the corporate expenditure restrictions. Mr. Bopp and the Center have been involved in a number of high profile challenges to campaign finance and disclosure laws including, *Citizens United, Wisconsin Right to Life v. FEC, RNC v. FEC,* and *Doe v. Reed.*

Former FEC Chairman Bradley Smith is the President of the Center for Competitive Politics which also reveals nothing regarding its sources of funding. The Center regularly files amicus briefs in major challenges to existing campaign finance laws and initiated *SpeechNow.org v. FEC* and *Ohio Right to Life v. Ohio Election Commission*.

Until the *Citizens United* decision, the litigation offensive undertaken by these groups, political parties, and others, to some extent, remained under the radar. This was because the cases were framed as narrow, seemingly technical legal challenges, and further, because the Roberts Court acted incrementally in undermining campaign finance laws in its first four years.

These groups pursued this litigation strategy for the simple reason that they were often challenging longstanding campaign finance laws that had *already* been upheld and declared constitutional. Until *Citizens United*, anti-reform groups would not challenge the general constitutionality of a campaign finance law "on its face," but instead would frame their cases as narrow challenges to the law "as applied" to specific situations.

These kinds of "as applied" challenges allowed the Roberts Court to significantly erode existing precedent without having to reverse such precedent explicitly. For instance, in its 2007 decision in *Wisconsin Right to Life v. FEC*, the Roberts Court effectively gutted several provisions of the Bipartisan Campaign Reform Act of 2002 (BCRA) without explicitly striking down the Act which had been previously upheld by the Supreme Court in *McConnell* just three years earlier.

More Overt Anti-Reform Measures

More recently, however, the conservative wing of the Supreme Court has become more overt in its hostility to existing campaign finance laws. Breaking with what Justice [Antonin] Scalia described as the "faux judicial restraint" that characterized its earlier decisions, the Supreme Court went out of its way to

Citizens United Defies Precedents and Common Sense

The [Supreme] Court's blinkered and aphoristic [pithy] approach to the First Amendment may well promote corporate power at the cost of the individual and collective self-expression the Amendment was meant to serve. It will undoubtedly cripple the ability of ordinary citizens, Congress, and the States to adopt even limited measures to protect against corporate domination of the electoral process. Americans may be forgiven if they do not feel the Court has advanced the cause of self-government today. . . .

In a democratic society, the longstanding consensus on the need to limit corporate campaign spending should outweigh the wooden application of judge-made rules. . . . The Court's opinion is thus a rejection of the common sense of the American people, who have recognized a need to prevent corporations from undermining self-government since the founding, and who have fought against the distinctive corrupting potential of corporate electioneering since the days of [former President] Theodore Roosevelt. It is a strange time to repudiate that common sense. While American democracy is imperfect, few outside the majority of this Court would have thought its flaws included a dearth of corporate money in politics.

Justice John Paul Stevens, "Opinion on Citizens United,
Appellant v. Federal Election Commission,"
Supreme Court of the United States, January 21, 2010.

order reargument in the case *Citizens United v. FEC* for the purpose of overturning two past Supreme Court decisions that had upheld corporate spending restrictions.

This development makes clear that opponents of campaign finance reform—and their ideological allies on the High Court—have far more ambitious goals than merely rolling back recent legal reforms instituted by BCRA. *Instead, their apparent goal is to go back nearly a century and dismantle many of the campaign finance reforms that have governed elections for decades, and to revert to the era of unregulated political spending that characterized the turn of the 20th Century.*

It is clear that even disclosure laws—which conservatives have long championed as the only legitimate form of campaign finance reform—are under attack.

James Bopp, the attorney who initiated *Citizens United* and a longtime member of the RNC, for instance, has made no secret of the fact that his ultimate goal is the elimination of virtually *all* campaign finance restrictions including the reporting of donors. In January, he told the *New York Times* that, "[g]roups have to be relieved of reporting their donors if lifting the prohibition on their political speech is going to have any meaning."

One disclosure case brought by Mr. Bopp—*Doe v. Reed*—was argued before the Supreme Court on April 28, 2010. *Doe v. Reed* does not address contributors, but rather the disclosure of referenda petition signatories in connection to a Washington state ballot referendum regarding domestic partnerships. But there are numerous cases that do seek to overturn contributor disclosure provisions in the lower courts. One such challenge was brought by Mr. Bopp on behalf of the inaptly named "Committee for Truth in Politics." This group is simultaneously suing the FEC to avoid disclosing its donors while spending millions of dollars airing factually unsupported attack ads against vulnerable candidates, for instance, calling the financial reform bill a "$4 trillion bailout for banks."

A Highly Litigious Era

As a result of this large-scale anti-reform effort, the campaign finance arena has experienced one of its most active litigation periods. In the past three years, the Campaign Legal Center, a nonpartisan Washington-based legal institute with particular expertise in issues of campaign finance law, lobbying regulation and government ethics, has represented a party or was active as an *amicus* [friend of the court] in over twenty-five cases in both federal and state court, and monitored and consulted in several additional cases. . . .

The ultimate goal of this multi-pronged attack on campaign finance law is to turn back the clock nearly a century and allow untraceable and unlimited contributions from and expenditures by those seeking favors from elected officials. Opponents of campaign finance laws believe they have a sympathetic Supreme Court that will allow them to ignore many decades' worth of High Court precedent, as well as public outrage and scandals running from "Teapot Dome" to Watergate.

To date, beyond the controversial and highly unpopular *Citizens United* decision, much of this well-orchestrated attack on campaign finance laws has escaped the notice of the press and the American people. At stake are not only millions of what could become "invisible dollars" spent on political campaigns but more importantly, the ability to use money to influence—if not determine—who controls the reins of power in this nation.

> "It's . . . premature to pin all the responsibility for the election spending boom on Citizens United. The rules that govern corporate- and union-funded advertising in 2010 were largely in place in 2008."

The Effects of the *Citizens United* Decision on Campaign Finance Reform Have Yet to Be Determined

Christopher Beam

Christopher Beam covers politics for Slate.com. In the following viewpoint, the author argues that, while there are reasons for concern about how much the Citizens United *ruling—a landmark decision by the US Supreme Court that states that corporate funding of independent political broadcasts in candidate elections cannot be limited—will affect election spending, the actual impact on spending and the possibility of corruption are as yet unknown. Political campaign expenditures tend to increase every four years naturally, Beam points out, so an increase following the* Citizens United *ruling is not necessarily attributable to the ruling itself. And, as Beam points out, the* Citizens United *decision did not change the disclosure laws that existed prior to 2010. Beam concludes that the* Citizens United *ruling will have negative effects on campaign finance reform, but its "practical" effects will remain unknown in the immediate future.*

As you read, consider the following questions:

1. According to the viewpoint, by how much have interest groups increased their spending on elections since 2006?

2. What 2007 Supreme Court ruling allowed corporations to fund political ads up to Election Day provided they did not endorse a specific candidate?

3. According to the viewpoint, what kind of organization is allowed to keep its donor list secret?

Democrats will find plenty of scapegoats for their electoral losses in 2010, but high on the list will be Supreme Court Chief Justice John Roberts. The *Washington Post* reported on Monday that interest groups have spent five times as much on this year's midterm elections as they did in 2006, and the money has gone overwhelmingly to Republicans—a spike that the *Post* says "is made possible in part by a series of Supreme Court rulings unleashing the ability of corporations and interest groups to spend money on politics."

Note the key phrase "in part." We know recent Supreme Court rulings—including this year's [2010] *Citizens United v. Federal Election Commission*, which opened the door for corporations and unions to spend unlimited amounts of their own treasury money (as opposed to forming a PAC [political action committee]) on broadcast endorsements—have changed the campaign finance game. We just don't know to what extent. Independent expenditures trend up every four years anyway, so we'd expect to see more outside spending in 2010 than in 2006, even without a landmark Supreme Court decision.

Much Remains the Same After *Citizens United*

[The] *Citizens United [v. Federal Election Commission* decision] probably doesn't really change Campaign Finance Law as much as everyone thinks it does. . . . To put it bluntly: the law regarding campaign finance was already pretty bad. Corporations could already, through the use of soft money, donate to whatever campaigns they wanted. . . . What *Citizens United* did was simply let corporations know that they no longer had to beat around the bush, they can now donate whatever they would like directly to a certain candidate.

Brian Turner, "*Citizens Divided on* Citizens United: *Campaign Finance Reform and the First Amendment,*" *Lawschoolblog.org, October 28, 2010.*

It's therefore premature to pin all the responsibility for the election spending boom on *Citizens United*. The rules that govern corporate- and union-funded advertising in 2010 were largely in place in 2008—an election that, while expensive, didn't spark the same suspicions of corporate manipulation. That year, the door for corporate spending in elections was already wide open. *Citizens United* just removed the hinges.

The Ban on Broadcast Campaign Ads

After the Bipartisan Campaign Finance Act [formally known as the Bipartisan Campaign Reform Act, or BCRA], better known as McCain-Feingold, passed in 2002, corporations and unions were banned from spending money on broadcast campaign ads in the one or two months before an election. (The "window" spans the 30 days before a primary and 60 days before a general [election].) The Supreme Court softened the ban with its 2007 decision in *Federal Election Commission v. Wisconsin Right to Life* ruling that corporations can fund ads right up to Election Day as long as the ads don't expressly endorse a candidate. For example, you can say, "Candidate X supports terrible policies that we disagree with," but you can't say, "Vote for Candidate X." (Corporations called these "issue ads." The FEC [Federal Election Commission] called them "sham issue ads" that simply provide a loophole for endorsements.) In 2008, therefore, corporations could already finance campaign ads as long as they weren't too specific.

Citizens United eliminated the ban altogether, and with it the distinction between "issue ads" and "express endorsements." Corporations and unions can now spend unlimited amounts of money on any kind of campaign ad they want, whenever they want. But the new landscape isn't all that different than it was in 2008. "They could spend the money before," says Brad Smith, a former FEC commissioner and a professor at Capital University Law School. "It just would have gone to issue ads run 60 days before an election. Now it goes to express advocacy."

The Disclosure Rules Remain the Same

So how much has *Citizens United* really influenced the rise in spending? It's hard to say. FEC reports are released monthly, so we won't be able to take full stock of corporate spending until after the election. But even then, not all groups that produce ads have to disclose their donors. *Citizens United* didn't change the disclosure rules for corporations and unions. But those that exercise their new spending liberties can avoid taking responsibility for their spending by exploiting pre-existing loopholes. For example, instead of spending money directly on an ad, which requires disclosure to the FEC, they give money to a 501(c)4 organization, which doesn't. (A 501(c)4 can keep its donors secret as long as its primary purpose is not campaigning.) These "shadowy" groups are nothing new. They're just more flush this year.

The frustration for campaign finance reformers is that *Citizens United* didn't have to happen the way it did. Originally, the court case was about disclosure rules, says Fred Wertheimer of Democracy 21. The court told the litigants to come back and rebrief the case to make it about the ban on corporate spending instead. "This case was actually brought by the five justices," says Wertheimer. "They wanted to rule on it." No doubt *Citizens United* set back the cause of campaign finance reform. But the jury is still out on its practical effects.

> *"Despite the president's strong rhetoric and a push by Obama and congressional Democrats to respond to the court's decision through legislation, no new law was passed . . . to limit the effects of the* Citizens United *decision."*

Campaign Finance Reform Is Still Necessary After the *Citizens United* Ruling

Kenneth P. Doyle

Kenneth P. Doyle is a campaign finance analyst for the Bureau of National Affairs (BNA), a news service for business and government professionals. In the following viewpoint, Doyle contends that, despite numerous setbacks on the reform agenda following the Supreme Court's January 2010 Citizens United *ruling, campaign finance reform remains vital to improving the election system. Doyle asserts that existing regulations have not prevented elections from depending on massive amounts of money, with small donors only accounting for 10 percent of total donations in the 2010 midterm elections. He argues that the failure to pass new legislation, and the reluctance of the Federal*

Kenneth P. Doyle, "BNA Money & Politics Report: 2010 Battle over *Citizens United* Ruling Still Unresolved as 2012 Campaign Looms," Democracy21.org, January 12, 2010. Copyright © 2010 by Bureau of National Affairs. Reproduced by permission.

Election Commission and Internal Revenue Service to enforce existing rules, will only encourage more spending in the future.

As you read, consider the following questions:

1. When did President Barack Obama criticize the *Citizens United* ruling?

2. What was the total amount of money spent on the 2008 presidential election, according to Doyle?

3. What percentage of the US population does Doyle maintain contributes $200 or more to campaigns?

If 2010 began with clear battle lines drawn over campaign finance policy due to the controversy over a high-profile Supreme Court ruling, 2011 starts out in a more uncertain landscape, with last year's policy debates still unresolved and a looming presidential election campaign cycle likely to shatter spending records.

Last January, President Obama put a spotlight on campaign finance in his annual State of the Union address with dramatic criticism of the Supreme Court's decision in *Citizens United v. Federal Election Commission* [a landmark decision that essentially states that corporate funding of independent political broadcasts in candidate elections cannot be limited].

The president blasted the court for striking down as unconstitutional decades-old restrictions on direct campaign spending by corporations and unions. The ruling, Obama said, would "open the floodgates for special interests—including foreign corporations—to spend without limit in our elections." As he spoke, Justice Samuel Alito, who supported the *Citizens United* decision, was seen shaking his head and mouthing the words "not so."

Despite the president's strong rhetoric and a push by Obama and congressional Democrats to respond to the court's decision through legislation, no new law was passed last year [2010] to limit the effects of the *Citizens United* decision.

It seems less likely that Obama will again highlight the issue in his 2011 State of the Union speech, expected Jan. 25.

Most observers agree that his favored legislative response—increasing disclosure of funding sources for groups that spend money on campaigns and clamping down on some types of corporate campaign spending—faces even dimmer prospects in the new 112th Congress than it did previously, when Democrats controlled both the House and Senate.

Also, some Democrats now suggest that groups supporting their candidates could raise more money in the next campaign to try to compete with the efforts of Republicans, who dominated the 2010 campaign season.

'Parallel Systems'

Yet, while the impact of the *Citizens United* decision still dominates campaign finance discussions a year later, not all regulations have been swept aside. Dollar limits on direct campaign contributions to federal candidates and political parties—as well as a ban on any direct corporate and union contributions to candidates and parties—remain intact, while most rules governing "independent" campaign spending have been swept aside by the courts.

The result, according veteran campaign reformer Fred Wertheimer, is that the United States increasingly has "parallel systems" of financing federal campaigns: the regulated, disclosed system for direct contributions to candidates and parties and the unlimited, largely undisclosed, and perhaps increasingly important independent campaign spending system used by outside political groups favoring particular candidates and parties.

Wertheimer insists that disclosure legislation can still be passed in the new Congress despite the failure of supporters to get their bill, known as the DISCLOSE [Democracy Is Strengthened by Casting Light on Spending in Elections] Act (H.R. 5175/S. 3628), passed so far. In a recent interview with

BNA [Bureau of National Affairs], he pointed to comments by key, moderate Republicans in the Senate indicating that they support the concept of disclosure and might vote to break a filibuster [an attempt to block or delay congressional action]. Wertheimer noted, as well, poll numbers showing consistent public support for disclosure and opposition to the Supreme Court's *Citizens United* ruling.

It remains unclear, however, how such public support could be translated into congressional action in the near future.

Even those lawmakers supporting the DISCLOSE Act last year—such as Senate Rules and Administration Committee Chairman Charles Schumer (D-NY) and Senate Majority Leader Harry Reid (D-NV)—have said little recently about whether or how they plan to revive campaign finance legislation. Campaign reformers also will miss a key Senate supporter for their cause in former senator Russ Feingold (D-WI), who was defeated in his 2010 re-election bid.

In the House, where the GOP gained majority control in the November elections, progress for campaign finance legislation could be even tougher, with traditional Republican opponents of most regulatory proposals taking over positions of power. For example, Rep. Dan Lungren (R-CA)has been installed as chairman of the House Administration Committee, which has jurisdiction over campaign finance issues. Lungren already has indicated he plans to steer the panel away from campaign finance proposals advanced by Democrats in the last Congress and toward GOP priorities, such as fighting risks of voting fraud.

Money Abundant in Regulated System

The campaign finance limits that remain intact after the *Citizens United* ruling include the $2,400 per-election limit on individual campaign contributions to a federal candidate and the $30,400 annual limit on individual contributions to national political parties. Those limits are due to be adjusted upward slightly for the 2012 election cycle to account for inflation. New contribution limits are expected to be announced in February [2011] by the Federal Election Commission.

Though contributions to candidates and parties are limited, those limits have not prevented candidate and party fund-raising from thriving within the regulated system, even without the unlimited party "soft money" banned by the 2002 Bipartisan Campaign Reform Act. Campaign money totals approached a total of $4 billion in the 2010 mid-term electron cycle—with the vast majority of the money still raised and spent by candidates, parties, and regulated political action committees. The total in the 2008 presidential election cycle topped $5 billion, when both major presidential candidates publicly discouraged campaign spending by outside groups seeking to influence the race.

Obama's own 2008 presidential campaign shattered previous records by raising $750 million in individual contributions. Obama supporters hailed the campaign's fund-raising as emblematic of the candidate's ability to motivate millions of contributors who gave relatively small amounts. The Obama campaign, however, also relied heavily on donors at the higher end of the scale—suggesting that even the regulated campaign contribution system is dominated by those wealthy enough and with a big enough stake in the political process to give thousands of dollars in contributions each year.

A study by the nonprofit Campaign Finance Institute published after the 2008 campaign was over found that about 34 percent of Obama's general election campaign funds came from donors who gave him no more than $200 for the general election. While that was a historically higher proportion of small donors than nearly all other major presidential campaigns, Obama still received most of his campaign money from bigger donors, including 42 percent of the campaign's total funds from those who gave $1,000 or more.

The dependence of federal campaigns on big donors was even more pronounced in the 2010 congressional campaigns, contravening a theory posited by some in 2008 that Obama's success in expanding the base of political donors—especially those giving small amounts via the internet—might signal a more fundamental change in the campaign financing system. Instead, in 2010 small donors in the less than $200 level provided only 10 percent of the total money raised by federal candidates and PACs, according to an analysis released by Americans for Campaign Reform. ACR, a nonprofit that advocates for a new system of public financing of congressional campaigns, found that donors at the other end of the scale, giving at least $2,300, provided nearly two-thirds of the total campaign funding in 2010.

The study also found that less than a quarter of 1 percent of the U.S. population made campaign contributions of $200 or more. Yet, this sliver of the American public provided 90 percent of the campaign money contributed in the mid-term elections.

Boom in Independent Spending

Even though fund-raising has continued to grow within the regulated system—and has continued to rely mainly on the nation's wealthiest individuals and interests—the current candidate and party limits continue to provide restraint on the amount of contributions coming from any single source. Meanwhile, reporting requirements for candidates and regulated political committees provide the public with information about who is funding each campaign.

On the other hand, campaign spending that is not closely coordinated with a candidate or party—as well as contributions to independent political groups spending money to influence campaigns—may now be on the way to almost complete deregulation. This trend seems bound to increase the importance of groups with bland names as American Cross-roads and American Action Network, some of which came from nowhere to become fund-raising juggernauts in 2010.

Constraints on campaign spending are diminishing rapidly in the wake of *Citizens United* and related court rulings. Congress failed to pass new legislation, while regulatory authorities—such as the Federal Election Commission and Internal Revenue Service—appear reluctant to impose new rules or take enforcement actions to curb political activities by independent entities. That means corporations, unions, and wealthy individuals have been freed to try to influence campaigns with far fewer legal constraints than they have faced in the past.

Even possible concerns about public reaction to the influence of controversial funding sources—for example hedge-fund operators, oil companies, or others who reportedly impacted the 2010 campaign—may be diminishing. That is because the public may not know much about such controversial funders, with major groups involved in last year's campaigns able to operate without providing information during the campaign season about their donors.

Whether or not Congress acts on any campaign finance proposals, a regulatory response could be still shaped by the FEC, which has long promised a new rulemaking to follow up on the *Citizens United* decision. Here again, however, the future is uncertain.

The six-member FEC is equally divided among Republican and Democratic commissioners, who appear to have fundamental disagreements about legal and constitutional questions and thus continue to disagree about how to respond to the recent court decisions. And, there appear to be no prospects on the horizon of any changes in the makeup of the FEC, which could impact the policy debate at the agency.

Total Contributions for 2012 May Skyrocket

With both candidate fund-raising and independent campaign spending poised to set possible spending records by the end of the current election cycle, the combined impact of the parallel campaign financing systems could elevate the total price tag of the next presidential campaign cycle far beyond previous levels, according to Wertheimer and other experts.

Obama campaign insiders, for example, reportedly believe his re-election effort can improve on the 2008 record and boost his funding total enough to become the first $1 billion candidate—a level that any Republican challenger to the president surely will attempt to match.

Meanwhile, congressional campaigns in 2012 may match or even exceed the record levels of the 2010. Congressional campaign funding will be boosted especially by Republican efforts to keep control of the House and gain control of the Senate—efforts that Democrats will certainly pull out all stops to resist. Democrats lost the House majority in the 2010 midterm elections but managed to hold onto the Senate. Yet, political observers have noted that Democrats face a higher hurdle in retaining their slim Senate majority in the next election; they must defend 23 incumbents' seats in 2012, while Republicans must hold only 10 Senate seats.

2010

On top of those efforts, outside groups were able to adapt quickly and take advantage of the *Citizens United* decision in early 2010 to spend enough to impact congressional elections just nine months later. The nonprofit watchdog Center for Responsive Politics said the total spending by outside groups reported to the FEC was almost $300 million, with funding sources of only about half of that money disclosed. Another watchdog group, the Campaign Finance Institute, estimated that total spending by outside groups (including that not re-

Citizens United Points to a Dark Future for Democracy

Did *Citizens United* matter? The answer is yes—significantly. And unless remedied, the ruling points toward a truly dystopian future, when candidates, campaigns, and parties are drowned out by special interest funding as loud as it is stealthy.

Michael Waldman,
"Supreme Court's Citizens United *Decision*
Will Warp Policymaking," U.S. News and World Report,
September 27, 2010.

quired under current rules to be reported to the FEC) may have been over $500 million for 2010, with the impact of outside groups' spending concentrated on the most closely contested, targeted races.

Some of the most high-profile groups spending in the 2010 campaign—such as the trio of Republican-leaning groups American Action Network, American Crossroads, and Crossroads GPS—did not even exist before the *Citizens United* decision was handed down a year ago. The groups—which have links to major Republican political figures, such as former White House aide Karl Rove and former Republican National Committee chairman Ed Gillespie—officially reported spending a total of nearly $60 million in last year's campaign and have acknowledged that they actually raised and spent millions more.

Now, with a full two years instead of a few months to adapt to the changed legal landscape, such outside groups may be poised to have an even bigger impact, experts say. Additionally, Democratic-leaning groups were somewhat subdued in 2010, due at least partly to the public stance of Obama and top congressional Democrats in opposition to the *Citizens United* ruling and its impact on campaign spending. That may not be the case in 2012, as many observers predict that Democratic-leaning groups will gear up to compete more effectively.

Reformers Not Giving Up

Despite the rising tide of campaign money on top of legislative and legal setbacks, campaign reformers like Wertheimer, president of the nonprofit group Democracy 21, said they are not about to give up the fight for tighter regulation of money in politics.

Wertheimer said reformers will continue to push for a pared-down version of the DISCLOSE Act, which focuses narrowly on making public the names of those funding shadowy campaign spending groups. He noted that Democrats had signaled earlier that they were willing to drop the restrictions on spending by companies with government contracts or foreign owners, which had been included in the original DISCLOSE Act.

Reformers also will continue to push for other proposals, including greater public financing of federal campaigns. Wertheimer, for example, long has advocated for revamping the current system for public financing of presidential campaigns, which is falling into disuse as top candidates are able to raise hundreds of millions of dollars in private contributions. Yet, public financing proposals, like other campaign finance legislation, appear to face an even tougher road in the 112th Congress than in they did in the past.

Arizona Case Challenges Public Financing

State public financing systems also have faced increasing opposition and have been challenged more and more in court in recent years by opponents of campaign finance regulations. The challenges include a case originating in Arizona that is now set to be argued before the U.S. Supreme Court at the end of March (*Arizona Free Enterprise Club's Freedom Club PAC v. Bennett*, U.S., No. 10-238 oral argument 3/28/2011).

The Arizona case centers on a "trigger provision" in that state's law which provided additional public funding to a candidate that faces increased spending by a privately financed opponent or an outside group. This type of provision is not central to all public financing schemes and a court ruling that such trigger provisions are unconstitutional would not be "a dagger" ending all types of public campaign financing systems, according to Wertheimer.

Of more concern, he indicated, is another case challenging provisions of Connecticut's public campaign financing law. But, the Supreme Court has not yet indicated if it will review the Connecticut case (*Green Party of Connecticut v. Lenge*, U.S., No. 10-795, cert. petition file 12/9/2010).

'Playing Defense'

While Wertheimer insists that it will be possible to get Congress to consider new campaign finance disclosure requirements in the months and years ahead, he also admitted that a major task facing reformers will be to simply hold onto those campaign regulations still left standing after the *Citizens United* decision. Primarily, this means fighting to hold onto contribution limits for candidates and parties in the face of demands to allow these regulated entities to raise more money to keep up with unregulated outside groups.

Another prominent campaign reformer, Craig Holman, of the nonprofit Public Citizen put it bluntly in a phone interview with *BNA*. "I fully understand I'm going to be playing defense for the next two years," said Holman, who has helped lobby for major campaign finance bills passed in recent years.

Despite the chilly political climate now faced by reformers, Holman suggested there may be opportunities to pursue some new reform ideas and even to enlist GOP support for those.

He indicated he plans to pursue ideas first floated last year to control special spending "earmarks"—a favorite target of conservatives. Holman's plan would require that entities receiving earmarked funding to refrain from playing a prominent role in providing campaign money to the lawmaker sponsoring the earmark.

Another area of possible renewed interest would be to codify and beef up ethics rules in the executive branch, Holman said. He suggested that House Republicans interested in pursuing more aggressive oversight of the Obama administration could have an interest in examining whether the ethics rules for executive agencies are as strict as tougher congressional rules on such items as gifts and travel, which were adopted as part of the 2007 Honest Leadership and Open Government Act.

Party Limits Challenged

Holman, Wertheimer and others have suggested ther biggest challenge may be resisting calls to lift current limits on national political parties. Control on party funding—through elimination of unlimited soft money contributions—was the central clement of BCRA, the last major campaign reform bill passed nearly a decade ago.

Proposals to ease current barriers on parties—including controls on what a party may spend to did individual candidates—have long been a prime target of opponents of campaign regulation. There have been a number of proposals to have Congress change the law in this area and a related legal challenge now may be considered by the Supreme Court.

Lawyers for the Republican National Committee and former representative Anh "Joseph" Cao (R-LA) in December asked the Supreme Court to review a constitutional challenge to limits on contributions and coordinated spending by a political party on behalf of its federal candidates (*Cao v. FEC*, US, No. 10-776, cert. petition filed 12/6/10). The bid for Supreme Court review came after a divided federal appeals court in New Orleans rejected last year a challenge to FEC rules on party spending brought by the RNC and Cao.

Campaign Regulation Opponents Invigorated

While campaign reformers may have to play defense for awhile, longtime opponents of campaign finance regulation have been emboldened by the *Citizens United* ruling and other recent court decisions. Those advocates—who have long argued that campaign regulations are antithetical to free speech—are seeking to push their cause even further in 2011 and beyond.

A series of new legal challenges of state campaign finance rules has been launched in courts across the country. At the same time, a conservative nonprofit group in Washington—the Center for Competitive Politics (CCP)—has put forward a policy agenda calling for Congress to loosen the remaining restraints on contributions to candidates and parties.

The CCP in December highlighted a list of a half-dozen specific proposals for loosening current regulations, including removing limits on party spending in coordination with candidates, as well as raising existing individual contribution limits.

In addition, the group proposed restoring federal tax credits for smaller campaign contributions. A tax credit of up to $100 existed prior to federal tax reform laws passed in 1986, CCP noted, and the credit could be worth even more if adjusted for inflation from the time it was first put into place in 1978. The idea of such a tax credit traces back to a campaign finance commission launched by President [John F.] Kennedy in the 1960s, and still has value as a way to encourage smaller contributions and public involvement in the political process, CCP suggested. . . .

"Advocates for the antiquated system of speech regulation rely on a worldview where only politicians, the media, and a few favored interests should have a meaningful say in politics and campaigns."

The Best Approach to Campaign Finance Reform Is Less Regulation

Sean Parnell

Sean Parnell is the president of the Center for Competitive Politics, a nonpartisan, nonprofit group that advocates for the protection of First Amendment rights. In the following viewpoint, Parnell maintains that the campaign donation system can be reformed with several simple changes that will update it for the twenty-first century, including eliminating limits on spending, raising donation limits, and reinstating tax credits for donations up to $100. Parnell asserts that such changes would more accurately reflect the political and economic realities of America.

As you read, consider the following questions:

1. According to the viewpoint, what court case struck down the limits on what citizens can give to politically inclined independent groups?

2. What group published a report outlining modern reform, according to the author?

3. What year did Congress last adjust for inflation the amounts for small donation tax credits?

While pundits continue to sort out the real meaning of last week's [November 2010] elections, some facts seem crystal clear: the United States held elections, millions of citizens voted for (or against) candidates as they saw fit, and, the candidates they chose will spend at least a couple of years in public service until the next election.

This obvious statement seems necessary given all of the hysteria and hyperbole in the wake of the U.S. Supreme Court's decision in *Citizens United v. Federal Election Commission [FEC]*, which said that corporations, unions, advocacy groups, and other associations have a First Amendment right to speak on behalf of their members, shareholders, and donors. Combined with another important case called *SpeechNow.org v. FEC*, which struck down limits on what citizens can give to independent groups that want to speak about politics, the self-styled campaign finance reform community predicted the end of democracy as we know it.

Instead, voters were exposed to vast quantities of political speech from a wide variety of perspectives and interests, speech with which they could agree or disagree—and speech they could affirm or discard.

Despite the fact that America's political system thrived in 2010, predictable calls to return to the old way of regulating political speech persist. Advocates for the antiquated system of speech regulation rely on a worldview where only politicians, the media, and a few favored interests should have a meaning-ful say in politics and campaigns.

They are pushing for taxpayer dollars to be directly handed to politicians running for office, a constitutional amendment to rip freedom of political speech out of the Bill of Rights, and a restoration of the old order by placing government bu-reaucrats back in charge of who is allowed to speak in politics, how often, to whom, in what manner, and what can be said.

Fortunately, First Amendment skeptics are unlikely to suc-ceed. The new Republican majority in the U.S. House seems to have little interest in reversing *Citizens United* or dishing out public money to politicians, nor does a strengthened Re-publican minority in the Senate. That's not to say Republicans have any sort of ideological purity on this issue—McCain-Feingold [formally known as Bipartisan Campaign Reform Act (BCRA)] passed in a Republican House and was signed by a Republican President—but it seems clear that the incoming Republican House majority will reject any onerous campaign finance laws.

The old "reform" agenda seems dead, undone by a First Amendment-friendly Supreme Court, opposition party success in the midterm elections, and a public that is largely indiffer-ent to stricter regulations.

But there is still an opportunity to address campaign fi-nance issues, including dealing with issues created by *Citizens United* or left over from previous "reform" legislation. Today, the Center for Competitive Politics released "After 2010: A Modern Agenda for Campaign Finance Reform," which out-lines steps policymakers can take to increase incentives for citizen participation in politics, encourage electoral competi-tion and simplify the maze of campaign finance regulations.

Many of these issues could have broad appeal on both sides of the aisle, and in some cases even generate some sup-port from the professional reform lobby. Here's a summary of a few of the issues that Congress should consider:

Reform Weakens National Parties' Messages

The voices of the national parties, now subjected to the McCain-Feingold limits, and candidates, operating under strict donation caps, are increasingly drowned out. "I approved this message" (a McCain-Feingold requirement) is a joke when it applies only to advertising produced by the candidate, a fraction of what voters actually watch.

Nina Easton,
"The Absurdity of Campaign Finance Reform,"
CNNMoney.com, October 29, 2010.

Eliminate Caps on Expenditures

Right now parties are severely limited in the amount of money they can spend on ads coordinated with their own candidates. This forces political parties to guess what issues and points their candidates would like communicated to their voters, and can often lead to candidates actually being hurt more than helped by their own parties. It seems silly to limit what parties can talk about with their own candidates, and that these limits serve some sort of anti-corruption purpose.

Raise Campaign Contribution Limits

There is little dispute that *Citizens United* and *SpeechNow.org* have both put candidates and political parties at a significant disadvantage to independent groups in terms of not just financial resources that can be raised, but the amount of time required to raise them. Simply put, independent groups face no limits and can literally raise millions of dollars with just a few phone calls, while candidates and parties must invest substantial amounts of time and resources in order to raise funds in dramatically lower increments. Simply increasing contribution limits to reflect inflation since 1974, when limits were first imposed, would have meant in 2010 that individuals would be able to contribute about $4,400 to candidates and $177,000 to political parties, and PAC [political action committee] limits to candidates would be roughly $22,000.

Restore Tax Credits for Small Contributions

Prior to the federal tax reform of 1986, taxpayers received a tax credit for political contributions up to $50, or $100 on a joint return. Adjusted for inflation from 1978 (the last time Congress changed the amounts), that credit today would be $165, or $330 for a joint return. Restoring the tax credit at adjusted levels would encourage contributions, increase the pool of small donations available to candidates, and make fundraising easier and less time consuming. In addition, a tax credit might encourage more people to become involved in campaigns and could do far more than contribution limits to restore faith in the political process.

Most of these proposals might not please the most obsessive First Amendment skeptics, who remain focused on limiting the quantity and variety of political speech and speakers. But several prominent "reformers" have already expressed interest in ideas like eliminating the cap on coordinated expenditures and tax credits for small contributions, and there is reason to believe that a bipartisan consensus could be built around these reforms.

It's time to abandon the old paradigm of campaign finance regulation, which was built on the notion that the desire of citizens to contribute to candidates and causes could be tightly limited and controlled, independent voices could be stifled, and that a reduction in corruption and an increase in the public's faith in government would result.

Instead, Congress should take this opportunity to modernize campaign finance regulation by increasing or removing limits that put candidates and parties at a significant disadvantage to business corporations, unions and advocacy groups.

Periodical Bibliography

The following articles have been selected to supplement the diverse views presented in this chapter.

Michael Crowley — "Campaign-Finance Reformers Survey the Wreckage," *Time*, October 21, 2010.

Stan Greenberg, Andrew Baumann, and Jesse Contario — "Strong Campaign Finance Reform: Good Policy, Good Politics," Common Cause, Change Congress and the Public Campaign Action Fund, February 8, 2010.

Alexandra Gutierrez — "Joe Miller, Campaign Finance Reform Advocate?" *American Prospect*, October 29, 2010.

Richard L. Hasen — "The FEC Is as Good as Dead," Slate.com, January 25, 2011.

Suzy Khimm — "'Campaign Finance Reform Is on Its Last Legs,'" *Mother Jones*, September 13, 2010.

Andy Kroll — "Dems Eye Legal Attack on Shadow Spending Groups," *Mother Jones*, January 28, 2011.

Ruth Marcus — "Campaign Finance Reform Will Fix Sleaze," RealClearPolitics.com, June 2, 2010.

John Samples — "Politics as the Friend of Campaign Finance Reform," *Cato Unbound*, November 30, 2010.

Bradley A. Smith — "The Myth of Campaign Finance Reform," *National Affairs*, Winter 2010.

Mary Theroux — "Fat Cats, Big Dogs, and Campaign Finance Reform," *The Independent Institute*, January 4, 2011.

Jonathan Turley — "Real Political Reform Should Go Beyond Campaign Finance," *Los Angeles Times*, February 11, 2010.

OPPOSING
VIEWPOINTS®
SERIES

CHAPTER 4

How Does the *Citizens United* Decision Affect Constitutional Rights?

Chapter Preface

The question of whether or not corporations qualify as persons—"corporate personhood," as it is known—under the law is a matter of controversy unique to the United States. An 1886 case before the US Supreme Court, *Santa Clara County v. Southern Pacific Railroad*, incidentally addressed corporate personhood when the court reporter, a former head of the Newburgh and New York Railway Company named J.C. Bancroft Davis, recorded a comment made by one of the justices of the court stating that all of the justices were in agreement that corporations were indeed to be accorded the same legal status as persons under the Fourteenth Amendment. Although the comment was made prior to the opening statements of the case, its sentiment came to be considered a form of judicial precedent. Three years later, in *Minneapolis and St. Louis Railroad Company v. Beckwith*, the Supreme Court explicitly ruled that corporations were persons with rights to due process and equal protection. And in the 1893 case *Noble v. Union River Logging Railroad Company*, the high court for the first time spelled out that corporations were covered under the Constitution's first ten amendments—the Bill of Rights—including the rights to life, liberty, and property. Following the contentious presidential election of 1904, Theodore Roosevelt was accused of accepting money from corporations to fund his campaign. In response, Roosevelt vowed to end corporate contributions to political campaigns. The result was the passage in 1907 of the Tillman Act, banning all corporate monetary donations to federal campaigns. In the 1936 case *Grosjean v. American Press Company*, the court decided that First Amendment rights extended to incorporated newspapers, which had been subject to a special tax if their circulation was more than 20,000. The court struck down the tax, ruling that it was an infringement of the right to free speech.

Although the notion of corporate personhood has been challenged numerous times since the 1890s, in general the Supreme Court has been friendly to corporations in this regard. In 1947, Congress passed the Labor-Management Relations Act, more commonly known as the Taft-Hartley Act. Aimed specifically at unions but also covering corporations overall, Taft-Hartley banned for the first time all incorporated bodies from contributing to federal political campaigns, but it also increased the right to free speech of corporations by granting them more control over their unionized employees and curbing union members' right to free association. Cases in 1967 and 1970 further expanded corporations' rights to include coverage under the Fourth and Seventh Amendments, respectively. Then beginning in 1976 the Supreme Court heard a series of cases that granted First Amendment protections to corporations, beginning with *Buckley v. Valeo*, which was brought in response to the passage of the Federal Election Campaign Act of 1971 and its 1974 amendments. In *Buckley v. Valeo*, the court held that limits on campaign contributions were constitutionally valid, but it also maintained that money donated to political campaigns is a protected form of speech. In the 1978 decision in *First National Bank of Boston v. Belotti*, the court went further, ruling that, under the First Amendment, corporate funds could be used to influence the outcome of political elections. On the other hand, in the 1990 case *Austin v. Michigan Chamber of Commerce*, the court decided that the limits set on corporate campaign donations by the Michigan Campaign Finance Act did not violate corporations' First or Fourteenth Amendment rights.

So the Supreme Court's January 2010 decision on the *Citizens United v. Federal Election Commission* case in favor of the idea of corporate personhood and First Amendment protection was not without judicial or cultural precedent. In fact, the differences between "natural" and "artificial" persons have been debated in the United States for more than a century, beginning with the rise of wealth, industrialism, and the business class in the mid to late nineteenth century. Opponents of the definition of corporations as persons argue that imbuing them with personhood, in addition to all the other legal and financial advantages they possess, gives corporations far too much power and diminishes the economic and political power of natural persons. Supporters maintain that there is enough legal distinction to prevent an imbalance of power. Questions from American University professor of constitutional law Jamin B. Raskin summarized the problem for the Public Broadcasting Service program *NOW*: "Is corporate personhood an all-or-nothing proposition? Can due process property protections attach to stock without corporate managers also enjoying the right to become political kingmakers with corporate treasuries?"

In the following chapter, viewpoint authors debate the effects of the *Citizens United* decision on the right to free speech afforded to American citizens under the First Amendment to the US Constitution.

"The Citizens United *ruling is rooted in the First Amendment. That is its basis, its only basis."*

The First Amendment Does Not Limit the Right to Free Speech to Only Individual Citizens

Floyd Abrams

Floyd Abrams is an attorney, an expert in Constitutional law, and the William J. Brennan Jr. Visiting Professor at Columbia University's Graduate School of Journalism. In the following viewpoint, Abrams holds that critics of the Citizens United v. Federal Election Commission *ruling who focus on any factor other than the First Amendment implications have little understanding of either the case or the amendment. Abrams asserts that the case was fundamentally about the question of whether money has a corrupting influence on the political process and whether monetary contributions are a protected form of political speech. The author writes that he was surprised, therefore, by the widespread response to the Supreme Court's decision from commentators, most of whom misunderstood the main points of the case, which Abrams explains by summarizing the arguments of the attorneys. Essentially, says Abrams, the case came down to the question of whether or not pointed materials could be banned under Citizens United. The court's ruling therefore was a rejection of First Amendment infringement.*

As you read, consider the following questions:

1. According to the viewpoint, what was the name of the first legislation that prevented corporations and unions from using money to affect political influence?

2. What two cases, as noted by Abrams, questioned the constitutionality of that legislation?

3. What act by government did the Supreme Court ultimately hope to prevent with the *Citizens United* decision?

Testifying before the Senate Judiciary Committee regarding her confirmation as a Supreme Court Justice, Solicitor General Elena Kagan summed up in a cool and even-handed manner the arguments she and her opponents in the *Citizens United v. FEC* [Federal Election Commission] case had made to the Supreme Court. The "strongest argument of the government," she said, "was the very substantial record that Congress put together" demonstrating that money spent by corporations and unions "could have substantial corrupting effect on the political process."

On the other side of the case, she recalled, there were "certainly strong arguments," in particular "that political speech is the highest form of speech under the First Amendment entitled to the greatest protection and that the courts should be wary of Congress regulating in this area in such a way as to protect incumbents to help themselves." Those, she repeated, "are strong arguments."

That summary, neatly encapsulating two rounds of oral arguments, briefs of the parties, fifty-four briefs amicus curiae, and hundreds of pages of judicial opinions in the ruling, bears little resemblance to most of the far more overheated and often overwrought descriptions of the case offered to the public.

I wasn't surprised by what seems to have been the general disapproval of the ruling. Campaign finance "reform" is generally viewed as an unmitigated good and is normally uncritically praised in publications and in the public statements of politicians. So a decision of the Supreme Court holding unconstitutional major elements of legislation ostensibly drafted to help take money out of politics was never going to be popular.

The Critics Overreacted

What I was less prepared for was the fury of critics of the opinion and the fierceness of their criticism. The ruling was treated as a desecration. How often, after all, does a scholar of such extraordinary distinction as Ronald Dworkin simply refuse to entertain the possibility that the Court—right or wrong—meant what it said? But for Dworkin, the Court's ruling was not only unpersuasive, not only wrong-headed, but was written in bad faith. It resulted not from some sort of failure of analysis but either from the Court's "instinctive favoritism of corporate interests" or its desire to favor the Republican Party. One of the nation's leading scholars on election law, Richard L. Hasen, was little more restrained, describing a line of the ruling as sounding "more like the rantings of a right-wing talk show host than the rational view of a justice with a sense of political realism." And then there were the journalists, typified by CNN's Jeffrey Toobin, who characterized the opinion as resting on "bizarre legal theories," and *Newsweek*'s Howard Fineman, who dismissed the decision as "one of the more amazing pieces of alleged jurisprudence that I've ever read." The *New York Times*, in separate editorials, excoriated the ruling as "disastrous," "terrible," and "reckless."

I was still less prepared for something else. The *Citizens United* ruling is rooted in the First Amendment. That is its basis, its only basis. But critics of the ruling often chose not to respond to—sometimes not even to mention—Justice [Anthony M.] Kennedy's First Amendment analysis in the majority opinion at all, as if the Court had simply ruled that Congress had passed a law with which it emphatically disagreed and would therefore strike down. President [Barack] Obama, a former professor of constitutional law, denounced the ruling when it was released and then again in his State of the Union speech without even adverting to the Court's reliance on the First Amendment. The *Nation* magazine published a five-page editorial condemning the ruling and urging adoption of a constitutional amendment to overturn it without even mentioning its First Amendment roots. And E.J. Dionne, Jr., in five columns published in the *Washington Post* both before and after the ruling, first warned of and then denounced the Court's "astonishing display of judicial arrogance, overreach and unjustified activism." He referred to the First Amendment only once in the five articles, characterizing "[d]efenders" of the ruling as "piously claim[ing] it's about 'free speech.'"

It is not as if the facts of the case could lead someone even vaguely knowledgeable about the First Amendment to recoil from its citation. Citizens United is a conservative group partially funded by corporate grants. It prepared a documentary denouncing in the harshest terms then-Senator Hillary Clinton when she was considered the front-runner for the Democratic nomination for President in 2008. The organization sought to show the documentary on Video-on-Demand during one of the late-campaign "blackout periods" during which the Bipartisan Campaign Reform Act of 2002 (BCRA) banned independent expenditures by corporations or unions supporting or opposing the election of candidates on television, cable, or satellite. To rely on the First Amendment to defend the speech of an ideologically charged group that sought to affect the choice of the next President hardly seems a stretch.

The Legality of Taft-Hartley Questioned

Nor had Justice Kennedy conjured up a First Amendment argument not before articulated. The first law to bar corporations and unions from using their funds to make independent expenditures designed to affect federal elections was the Taft-Hartley Act [named after Senator Robert Taft and Representative Fred A. Hartley Jr.; formally known as the Labor-Management Relations Act], adopted in 1947. Contributions by corporations to candidates had been barred since 1907, but not until the adoption of Taft-Hartley were *independent* expenditures—that is, money spent supporting a candidate in a manner uncoordinated with him or her—deemed criminal. From its adoption, the constitutionality of the statute was viewed as dubious. President Harry S. Truman vetoed the bill on the ground that it was a "dangerous intrusion on free speech."

The constitutionality of the new provisions was quickly questioned by the Supreme Court in *United States v. CIO [Congress of Industrial Organizations]*, in which the Court concluded that unless read extremely narrowly, "the gravest doubt would arise in our minds as to [the statute's] constitutionality." In that case and in the Court's later ruling in *United States v. Automobile Workers*, the more liberal members of the Court concluded that the statute was facially inconsistent with the First Amendment. In the former case, Justices [Wiley] Rutledge, [Hugo] Black, [William] Douglas, and [Frank] Murphy, probably the four most liberal jurists ever to sit on the Supreme Court at the same time, concluded that whatever "undue influence" was obtained by making large expenditures was outweighed by "the loss for democratic processes resulting from the restrictions upon free and full public discussion." In

Big Government Is to Blame, Not Big Money

The proper answer to large expenditures for speech is either more speech or, if the existing system proves unworkable, a constitutional amendment. As for money, it's just a symptom. We have a big money problem because we have a big government problem. By restraining the regulatory and redistributive powers of the state, we can minimize the influence of big money. Restoring the Framers' notion of enumerated, delegated, and limited federal powers will get government out of our lives and out of our wallets. That's the best way to end the campaign-finance racket, and root out corruption without jeopardizing political speech.

Robert A. Levy,
"Campaign Finance Reform: A Libertarian Primer,"
FindLaw.com, July 28, 2010.

the *Automobile Workers* case, a dissenting opinion by Justice Douglas (joined by Chief Justice [Earl] Warren and Justice Black) even more clearly presaged the later ruling of Justice Kennedy in *Citizens United*, concluding:

Some may think that one group or another should not express its views in an election because it is too powerful, because it advocates unpopular ideas, or because it has a record of lawless action. But these are not justifications for withholding First Amendment rights from any group—labor or corporate. . . . First Amendment rights are part of the heritage of all persons and groups in this country. They are not to be dispensed or withheld merely because we or the Congress thinks the person or group is worthy or unworthy.

The Decision Was Based on
Two Theories of Law

Justice Kennedy's analysis was rooted in two well-established legal propositions. The first, that political speech—not to say political speech about whom to vote for or against—is at the core of the First Amendment, is hardly novel. First Amendment theorists have occasionally debated how far beyond political speech the Amendment's protection should be understood to go, but there has never been doubt that generally, as Justice Kennedy put it, "political speech must prevail against laws that would suppress it, whether by design or inadvertence." Nor has it been disputed that the First Amendment "has its fullest and most urgent applications to speech uttered during a campaign for political office."

The second critical prong of Justice Kennedy's opinion addressed the issue of whether the fact that Citizens United was a corporation could deprive it of the right to endorse candidates by making independent expenditures that individuals had long since been held to have. In holding that the corporate status of an entity could not negate this right, Justice Kennedy cited twenty-five cases of the Court in which corporations had received full First Amendment protection. Many of them involved powerful newspapers owned by large corporations; others involved nonpress entities such as a bank, a real estate company, and a public utility company. Justice [John Paul] Stevens's dissenting opinion (but not most of the published criticism of the *Citizens United* ruling) took no issue with this historical record, acknowledging that "[w]e have long since held that corporations are covered by the First Amendment."

The inherent First Amendment dangers of any statute barring close-to-election speech advocating the election or defeat of candidates for office were starkly illustrated during questioning by the Justices of counsel for the United States. BCRA itself only applied to broadcast, cable, and satellite. But the logic of the government's position appeared to lead inexorably to the proposition that books as well could constitutionally be banned if funded by corporations or unions at times close to a primary or election. Deputy Solicitor General [Malcolm] Stewart, representing the government in March of 2010, did his best to avoid that issue but finally—and honorably—gave up the ghost:

> JUSTICE KENNEDY: Just to make it clear, it's the government's position that under the statute, if this [K]indle device where you can read a book which is campaign advocacy, within the 60–30 day period, if it comes from a satellite, it's under—it can be prohibited under the Constitution and perhaps under this statute?
>
> MR. STEWART: It—it can't be prohibited, but a corporation could be barred from using its general treasury funds to publish the book and could be required to use—to raise funds to publish the book using its PAC [political action committee].

And then this:

> CHIEF JUSTICE [JOHN G.] ROBERTS: Take my hypothetical. [A book] doesn't say at the outset. It funds—here is—whatever it is, this is a discussion of the American political system, and at the end it says vote for X.
>
> MR. STEWART: Yes, our position would be that the corporation could be required to use PAC funds rather than general treasury funds.
>
> CHIEF JUSTICE ROBERTS: And if they didn't, you could ban it?
>
> MR. STEWART: *If they didn't, we could prohibit the publication of the book using the corporate treasury funds.*

The Question of Banning Books

On reargument five months later, then-Solicitor General Kagan was well prepared to deal with the uproar that followed Stewart's response. She did so by seeking to draw a different line, arguing that while one section of the statute at issue, which also limited corporate and union expenditures, could cover "full-length books," there would be a "quite good as-applied challenge" were it used in that manner. Here was her best shot in response to a question she surely anticipated, more than any other: could books be banned under the government's theory or not?

> GENERAL KAGAN: [W]e took what the Court—what the Court's—the Court's own reaction to some of those other hypotheticals [about books] very seriously. We went back, we considered the matter carefully, and the government's view is that although 441b does cover full-length books, that there would be [a] quite good as-applied challenge to any attempt to apply 441b in that context. And I should say that the FEC has never applied 441b in that context. So for 60 years a book has never been at issue.

> JUSTICE [ANTONIN] SCALIA: What happened to the over-breadth doctrine? I mean, I thought our doctrine in the [First] Amendment is if you write it too broadly, we are not going to pare it back to the point where it's constitutional. If it's overbroad, it's invalid. What has happened to that[?]

> GENERAL KAGAN: I don't think that it would be substan-tially overbroad, Justice Scalia, if I tell you that the FEC has never applied this statute to a book. To say that it doesn't apply to books is to take off, you know, essentially nothing.

> CHIEF JUSTICE ROBERTS: But we don't put our—we don't put our First Amendment rights in the hands of FEC bu-reaucrats; and if you say that you are not going to apply it to a book, what about a pamphlet?

> GENERAL KAGAN: I think a—*a pamphlet would be differ-ent. A pamphlet is pretty classic electioneering, so there is no attempt to say that 441b only applies to video and not to print.*

I offer no critical comment about either advocate for the government. Both did precisely what the best Supreme Court advocates attempt to do when confronted with questions that expose the weakest link in their argument—try to avoid answering directly and then, when necessary, answer directly. Both were candid with the Court, Stewart conceding that the government's position on the constitutionality of the statute could justify as well a ban on books and Kagan acknowledging that the text of one relevant section of law already covered books. But their answers—the earlier seeking to provide constitutional justification for the banning of books, the latter attempting the same with respect to pamphlets—are hopeless. No relevant constitutional distinction can be drawn between books and pamphlets, and no distinction in this area between both books and pamphlets and broadcast and cable makes any sense at all.

What About Newspapers?

Did Justice Stevens and the other dissenters really believe that but for a congressionally drafted media exception such as was set forth in BCRA, newspapers owned by large corporations could be held criminally liable for endorsing candidates for federal office? Did they believe that the First Amendment would permit corporations or unions to be categorically banned from distributing books or pamphlets endorsing or damning candidates for the presidency? Or that Time Warner could produce the same documentary as had Citizens United, with the first protected by the First Amendment and the second unprotected? We cannot know because the dissenting opinion does not tell us. What we do know is that the dissenters voted to sustain a ruling holding that a political documentary seeking to persuade the public that Hillary Clinton was unfit to be elected President could be treated as criminal.

I do not suggest that no difficult issues are raised in this area. The determination of what constitutes "corruption" in a political context is difficult. The dangers of unrestricted corporate spending drowning out the voices of others may seem unlikely ones to me, but they certainly cannot be discounted out of hand. Nor can it be denied that the potential remains for some increase in what is referred to as "the appearance of corruption" as a result of vastly increased corporate or union involvement in electoral politics—if that, in fact, occurs. While my own views, like those expressed by Justice Kennedy in an earlier case, would protect political speech categorically against both of the latter interests, I can understand how views of others may differ. What I find inexplicable is the willingness of so many not even to acknowledge, let alone weigh, the powerful First Amendment interests at all. . . .

> *"Corporations . . . are inherently not the same as individuals and thus cannot have the same protections as individuals."*

The Free Speech of Corporations Is Not Guaranteed Under the First Amendment

Supreet Minhas

Supreet Minhas is a Columbia College student majoring in political science. In the following viewpoint, the author maintains that corporations are subject to the laws that govern the activities of the marketplace, not those that govern the activities of people. She suggests that the Citizens United v. Federal Election Commission *ruling—a landmark decision by the US Supreme Court that states that corporate funding of independent political broadcasts in candidate elections cannot be limited—will have unintended consequences for other business regulations. Because they have a distinct legal identity, Minhas argues, corporations do not have the same First Amendment rights as human beings. Nor do they need the same rights, Minhas says, because corpora-*

tions already possess an amount of wealth and influence beyond what individuals can obtain, in politics specifically through political action committees (PACs) and lobbyists. For Minhas, one of the possible side effects of classifying corporations as persons with protected rights is that it might muddy the government's ability to regulate other industries that might go on to equate money with speech.

As you read, consider the following questions:

1. According to the author, what is the legal difference between individuals and corporations?

2. What kinds of campaign donations could corporations make prior to the *Citizens United* ruling?

3. In what way does the author claim the *Citizens United* decision affects an independent judiciary?

In *Citizens United v. Federal Election Commission*, the U.S. Supreme Court overturned century-old restrictions on corporate spending in elections under the guise of protecting First Amendment free speech rights. Justice Anthony M. Kennedy, writing for the majority, said, "If the First Amendment has any force, it prohibits Congress from fining or jailing citizens, or associations of citizens, for simply engaging in political speech." This argument of the majority decision rests on the notions that corporations are covered by the same free speech protections as individual citizens and that campaign donations or financing are the same as speech.

Corporations, however, are inherently not the same as individuals and thus cannot have the same protections as individuals. There are a slew of laws that protect corporations and their interests in the arena for which they are by definition formed—namely the marketplace. The laws that govern corporations and the rights enjoyed by them are distinct from the laws and rights of individuals. A corporation, for example,

Copyright © 2010 by Tim Egan, Deep Cover and PoliticalCartoons.com.

can enter into contracts like an individual, but unlike an individual, a corporation's members can be protected by limited liability so their personal assets are not at stake.

The Restrictions Balance Power

If a corporation, then, is a distinct legal entity governed by different laws than an individual is, corporations are not protected under the First Amendment in the same way that individuals are protected. Corporations, especially in their most powerful and wealthy incarnations, are exponentially more influential than most individuals in America. The restrictions on corporate spending in elections that were overturned by the U.S. Supreme Court were meant to redress this power balance between average individuals and unduly influential businesses. Corporations already have a plethora of ways to influence politics, from political action committees to lobbyists on Capitol Hill. The framers of the Bill of Rights wanted to protect the voices of the trampled, not amplify the voices of the elite.

The other part of the Supreme Court's premise for its decision is that the First Amendment free speech clause applies to campaign funding. While speech can be interpreted loosely as any form of expression, such an open, ambiguous definition would create a myriad of problems with all kinds of laws. An architect has a vision of a building: it is his art, his self expression, yet he cannot ignore local zoning laws that, for instance, restrict the height of his building. Should he sue the state for violation of his free speech, his right to expression? Equating money with speech also opens the door to sundry ludicrous claims by, for instance, an employer who objects to minimum wage laws since he'd like to express that his employees are only worth paying $3 an hour. There have to be restrictions on what constitutes speech to prevent a bastardization of the term and an overly liberal interpretation of the First Amendment.

A corporation already has the power to issue a statement in favor of a candidate or policy through its political action committees, and individual members of a business are welcome to contribute money as well. However, allowing a corporation to use its vast profits to directly finance the election or to remove a candidate compromises the democratic notion of a free and fair election. There are unseemly ties even now between politicians and various industries, but this new ruling would make such connections more robust and give them a veneer of legitimacy. A politician financed by a business would become completely beholden to its political agenda and not to the voters.

An Independent Judiciary Is at Stake

It's not only the independence of politicians that's at stake, but also the independence of our judges, who are at the very least expected to be impartial. Many states still use elections to appoint judges, which leaves them vulnerable to the influence of political spending. In a recent speech at a law school conference, former Supreme Court Justice Sandra Day O'Connor worried about the impact of corporate campaign funding in judicial elections, saying that "judicial campaigning makes last week's decision in *Citizens United* an increasing problem for maintaining an independent judiciary."

Two cornerstones of our democracy—free elections and an independent judiciary—are threatened by the Supreme Court's activist and meddling decision. The case could have been decided much more narrowly in favor of *Citizens United*, but instead, the majority of the justices decided to expand the case to champion the rights of big money over the interest of the American people. Senators Dick Durbin (D-IL) and Arlen Specter (D-PA) introduced the Fair Elections Now Act last March [2009]. It would prohibit contributions from political action committees and would match individual donations, limited to $100, on a 4:1 basis so that fundraising focuses on the people. Such a system has been in place in New York City since the 1988 Campaign Finance Act. The rest of the country is long overdue to follow. Never before has the fight for public financing been more necessary.

> "A law that violates the Constitution can't be upheld because the law produces good outcomes (or because its invalidation would produce bad outcomes)."

Banning Corporate Campaign Contributions Is Unconstitutional

Glenn Greenwald

Glenn Greenwald was a constitutional and civil rights attorney before joining Salon.com as a political writer. In the following viewpoint, Greenwald admits that he takes issue with many aspects of the Citizens United v. Federal Election Commission *ruling, which essentially removes limits on corporate funding of independent political broadcasts in candidate elections, but he argues that laws cannot be enacted or repealed because of the possibility of their consequences but rather that they must be judged on their constitutionality. Greenwald finds most critics of the* Citizens United *ruling to be unpersuasive in their arguments against it, reviewing historical incidences of free-speech infringement in the name of desirable outcomes and finding them all lacking in reasoning. He goes on to suggest that he is skeptical of claims that* Citizens United *will open floodgates of unbridled corporate influence in American politics because he believes the system can hardly get worse, because current campaign finance legislation is weak and ineffective. As far as Greenwald is concerned, denying freedom of speech to unions, political advocacy groups, and corporations is the worst way to handle this problem.*

As you read, consider the following questions:

1. According to the author, on what single factor can the *Citizens United* ruling be rightfully judged?

2. To which groups other than corporations does the *Citizens United* decision apply?

3. What alternative means of financing elections does the author advocate?

The Supreme Court yesterday [January 21, 2010], in a 5-4 decision, declared unconstitutional (on First Amendment grounds) campaign finance regulations which restrict the ability of corporations and unions to use funds from their general treasury for "electioneering" purposes. The case, *Citizens United v. FEC* [Federal Election Commission], presents some very difficult free speech questions, and I'm deeply ambivalent about the court's ruling. There are several dubious aspects of the majority's opinion (principally its decision to invalidate the entire campaign finance scheme rather than exercising "judicial restraint" through a narrower holding). Beyond that, I believe that corporate influence over our political process is easily one of the top sicknesses afflicting our political culture. But there are also very real First Amendment interests implicated by laws which bar entities from spending money to express political viewpoints.

I want to begin by examining several of the most common reactions among critics of this decision, none of which seems persuasive to me. Critics emphasize that the Court's ruling will produce very bad outcomes: primarily that it will severely exacerbate the problem of corporate influence in our democracy. Even if this is true, it's not really relevant. Either the First Amendment allows these speech restrictions or it doesn't. In general, a law that violates the Constitution can't be upheld because the law produces good outcomes (or because its invalidation would produce bad outcomes).

One of the central lessons of the [President George W.] Bush era should have been that illegal or unconstitutional actions—warrantless eavesdropping, torture, unilateral Presidential programs—can't be justified because of the allegedly good results they produce (Protecting us from the Terrorists). The "rule of law" means we faithfully apply it in ways that produce outcomes we like and outcomes we don't like. Denouncing court rulings because they invalidate laws one likes is what the Right often does (see how they reflexively and immediately protest every state court ruling invalidating opposite-sex-only marriage laws without bothering to even read about the binding precedents), and that behavior is irrational in the extreme. If the Constitution or other laws bar the government action in question, then that's the end of the inquiry; whether those actions produce good results is really not germane. Thus, those who want to object to the Court's ruling need to do so on First Amendment grounds. Except to the extent that some constitutional rights give way to so-called "compelling state interests," that the Court's decision will produce "bad results" is not really an argument.

It Cannot Get Much Worse

More specifically, it's often the case that banning certain kinds of speech would produce good outcomes, and conversely, allowing certain kinds of speech produces bad outcomes (that's true for, say, White Supremacist or neo-Nazi speech, or speech advocating violence against civilians). The First Amendment is not and never has been outcome-dependent; the Government is barred from restricting speech—especially political speech—no matter the good results that would result from the restrictions. That's the price we pay for having the liberty of free speech. And even on a utilitarian level, the long-term dangers of allowing the Government to restrict political speech invariably outweigh whatever benefits accrue from such restrictions.

I'm also quite skeptical of the apocalyptic claims about how this decision will radically transform and subvert our democracy by empowering corporate control over the political process. My skepticism is due to one principal fact: I really don't see how things can get much worse in that regard. The reality is that our political institutions are already completely beholden to and controlled by large corporate interests ([US Senator] Dick Durbin [D-IL]: "banks own" the Congress). Corporations find endless ways to circumvent current restrictions—their armies of PACs [political action committees], lobbyists, media control, and revolving-door rewards flood Washington and currently ensure their stranglehold—and while this decision will make things marginally worse, I can't imagine how it could worsen fundamentally. All of the hand-wringing sounds to me like someone expressing serious worry that a new law in North Korea will make the country more tyrannical. There's not much room for our corporatist political system to get more corporatist. Does anyone believe that the ability of corporations to influence our political process was meaningfully limited before yesterday's issuance of this ruling?

I'm even more unpersuaded by the argument that this decision will "ensure that Republican candidates will be at an enormous advantage in future elections." What evidence is there for that? Over the past five years, corporate money has poured far more into the coffers of the Democratic Party than the GOP [Republican Party]—and far more into [Barack] Obama's campaign coffers than [John] McCain's (especially from Wall Street). If anything, unlimited corporate money will

Suppressing the Free Speech of Corporations Affects All Organizations

I think it's important to remember that "corporations" encompass much more than large, for-profit businesses. They also include a wide variety of non-profit and advocacy groups, including the ACLU [American Civil Liberties Union], the NRA [National Rifle Association], and NARAL [National Abortion Rights Action League], that are, by any reasonable definition, grassroots organizations advocating the views of large numbers of voters. Even if you think it's appropriate for Congress to regulate the speech of Exxon-Mobil and Pfizer, I think it's awfully hard to square the First Amendment with a law that limits the ability of NARAL or the NRA to advocate for its members' views.

Timothy B. Lee,
"Citizens United *and Corporate Money in Politics,*"
Cato@Liberty, *January 22, 2010.*

be far more likely to strengthen incumbents than either of the two parties (and unlimited union spending, though dwarfed by corporate spending, will obviously benefit Democrats more). Besides, if it were the case that this law restricts the ability of Republicans far more than Democrats to raise money in election cycles, doesn't that rather obviously intensify the First Amendment concerns?

Judicial Precedent Is Not Sacred

Then there's the always intellectually confused discussions of *stare decisis* [a legal term meaning that judges must obey the precedents set by earlier judges' decisions] and precedent. It's absolutely true that the *Citizens United* majority cavalierly tossed aside decades of judicial opinions upholding the constitutionality of campaign finance restrictions. But what does that prove? Several of the liberals' most cherished Supreme Court decisions did the same (*Brown v. Bd. of Education* rejected *Plessy v. Ferguson*; *Lawrence v. Texas* overruled *Bowers v. Hardwick*, etc.). Beyond that, the central principle which critics of this ruling find most offensive—that corporations possess "personhood" and are thus entitled to Constitutional (and First Amendment) rights—has also been affirmed by decades of Supreme Court jurisprudence; tossing that principle aside would require deviating from *stare decisis* every bit as much as the majority did here. If a settled proposition of law is sufficiently repugnant to the Constitution, then the Court is not only permitted, but required, to uproot it.

Ultimately, I think the free speech rights burdened by campaign finance laws are often significantly under-stated. I understand and sympathize with the argument that corporations are creatures of the state and should not enjoy the same rights as individuals. And one can't help but note the vile irony that Muslim "War on Terror" detainees have been essentially declared by some courts not to be "persons" under the Constitution, whereas corporations are.

But the speech restrictions struck down by *Citizens United* do not only apply to Exxon and Halliburton; they also apply to non-profit advocacy corporations, such as, say, the ACLU [American Civil Liberties Union] and Planned Parenthood, as well as labor unions, which are genuinely burdened in their ability to express their views by these laws. I tend to take a more absolutist view of the First Amendment than many people, but laws which prohibit organized groups of people—which is what corporations are—from expressing political views goes right to the heart of free speech guarantees no matter how the First Amendment is understood. Does anyone doubt that the facts that gave rise to this case—namely, the government's banning the release of a critical film about Hillary Clinton by Citizens United—is exactly what the First Amendment was designed to avoid? And does anyone doubt that the First Amendment bars the government from restricting the speech of organizations composed of like-minded citizens who band together in corporate form to work for a particular cause?

Campaign Finance Laws Are Ineffective

What is overlooked in virtually every discussion I've seen over the last 24 hours is how ineffective these campaign finance laws are. Large corporations employ teams of lawyers and lobbyists and easily circumvent these restrictions; wealthy individuals and well-funded unincorporated organizations are unlimited in what they can spend. It's the smaller non-profit advocacy groups whose political speech tends to be most burdened by these laws. Campaign finance laws are a bit like gun control statutes: actual criminals continue to possess large stockpiles of weapons, but law-abiding citizens are disarmed.

In sum, there's no question that the stranglehold corporations exert on our democracy is one of the most serious and pressing threats we face. I've written volumes on that very problem. Although I doubt it, this decision may very well worsen that problem in some substantial way. But on both pragmatic and Constitutional grounds, the issue of corporate influence—like virtually all issues—is not really solvable by restrictions on political speech. Isn't it far more promising to have the Government try to equalize the playing field through serious public financing of campaigns than to try to slink around the First Amendment—or, worse, amend it—in order to limit political advocacy?

There are few features that are still extremely healthy and vibrant in the American political system; the First Amendment is one of them, and the last thing we should want is Congress trying to limit it through amendments or otherwise circumvent it in the name of elevating our elections. Meaningful public financing of campaigns would far more effectively achieve the ostensible objectives of campaign finance restrictions without any of the dangers or constitutional infirmities. If yesterday's decision provides the impetus for that to be done, then it will have, on balance, achieved a very positive outcome, even though that was plainly not its intent.

> *"Ultimately . . . [the Citizens United]*
> *decision does far more than simply pro-*
> *vide Fortune 500 companies with a*
> *massive megaphone to blast their po-*
> *litical views to the masses; it also em-*
> *powers them to drown out any voices*
> *that disagree with them."*

Banning Corporate Campaign Donations Protects the Free Speech of Individuals

Ian Millhiser

Ian Millhiser, formerly an attorney for the National Senior Citizens Law Center's Federal Rights Project and assistant director for communications at the American Constitution Society, is a policy analyst at the Center for American Progress Action Fund. In the following viewpoint, Millhiser contends that the Citizens United ruling—a landmark US Supreme Court decision stating that corporate funding of independent political broadcasts in candidate elections cannot be limited—will increase the imbalance of political power between corporate interests and ordinary voters. According to Millhiser, the case was not at all about ex-

*tending First Amendment protections to unions, corporations, and nonprofit advocacy groups, which, Millhiser says, have always been free to express themselves through their political action committees (PACs) and lobbyists. The difference after Citi-*zens United, *writes Millhiser, is that corporations can use their company treasuries directly to influence political elections, which will create a fundamental imbalance between large-scale corporate donors and small, independent donors.*

As you read, consider the following questions:

1. According to the author, what means did corporations and organizations have to donate to campaigns prior to the *Citizens United* ruling?

2. How much money combined did the Barack Obama and John McCain campaigns spend during the 2008 presidential election, according to the viewpoint?

3. According to the author, how are legislators considering offsetting the effects of the *Citizens United* ruling?

In what could prove to be the most consequential Supreme Court decision in decades, all five of the Court's conservatives joined together today to invalidate a sixty-three year-old ban on corporate money in federal elections. In the process, the Court overruled a twenty year-old precedent permitting such bans on corporate electioneering; and it ignored the protests of the four more moderate justices in dissent. As Justice John Paul Stevens wrote for the dissenters:

> Today's decision is backwards in many senses. It elevates the majority's agenda over the litigants' submissions, facial attacks over as-applied claims, broad constitutional theories over narrow statutory grounds, individual dissenting opinions over precedential holdings, assertion over tradition, absolutism over empiricism, rhetoric over reality. Our colleagues have arrived at the conclusion that *Austin* must be

overruled and that §203 is facially unconstitutional only after mischaracterizing both the reach and rationale of those authorities, and after bypassing or ignoring rules of judicial restraint used to cabin the Court's lawmaking power.... *At bottom, the Court's opinion is thus a rejection of the common sense of the American people, who have recognized a need to prevent corporations from undermining self government since the founding,* and who have fought against the distinctive corrupting potential of corporate electioneering since the days of Theodore Roosevelt. It is a strange time to repudiate that common sense. *While American democracy is imperfect, few outside the majority of this Court would have thought its flaws included a dearth of corporate money in politics.*

The majority, for its part, claimed that corporate political spending must be protected to prevent "taking the right to speak from some and giving it to others," but they are simply wrong to claim that this is a case about free speech. Prior to *Citizens United*, no law prohibited anyone from saying anything they wanted. Corporate CEOs and other wealthy individuals could spend their own massive salaries to run political ads on TV. People who are less rich than corporate CEOs could pool their money together via organizations. The only thing that wasn't permitted before *Citizens United* is that the CEO of Bank of America could not tap into Bank of America's massive, multi-billion dollar treasury to defeat any lawmaker who thinks that TARP [Trouble Asset Relief Program] banks should pay back the federal government after it took expensive and unprecedented steps to prevent a total collapse of the U.S. banking system.

Ultimately, however, today's decision does far more than simply provide Fortune 500 companies with a massive megaphone to blast their political views to the masses; it also empowers them to drown out any voices that disagree with them. In 2008, the [Barack] Obama and [John] McCain campaigns combined spent just over $1.1 billion, an enormous, record-breaking sum at the time. $1.1 billion is nothing, however, compared to the billions of dollars in tax subsidies given to the oil industry every year, or the $117 billion fee President Obama wants to impose on the Wall Street bankers who created the Great Recession. Indeed, with hundreds of billions of dollars of corporate profits at stake every time Congress begins a session, wealthy corporations would be foolish not to spend tens of billions of dollars every election cycle to make sure that their interests are protected. No one, including the candidates themselves, has the ability to compete with such giant expenditures.

The good news is that lawmakers are already considering ways to mitigate the damage caused by *Citizens United*, and a number of options exist, such as requiring additional disclosures by corporations engaged in electioneering, empowering shareholders to demand that their investment not be spent to advance candidates they disapprove of, or possibly even requiring shareholders to approve a corporation's decision to influence an election before the company may do so. At the end of the day, however, many extremely well-moneyed corporations will still succeed in unleashing their treasuries on the electorate, and drowning out opposing voices.

"The money is coming in regardless of how much legislation is thrown at it. Therefore, the question then becomes whether or not we are willing to start denying fundamental rights in an effort to stop the cash."

The Constitutional Right to Free Speech Applies to All Americans, Including Corporations

Amy Schroder

Amy Schroder is a law clerk at the Orange County (California) District Attorney's Office West Justice Center and a contributor to the Nexus Journal. *In the following viewpoint, Schroder argues that the response to the* Citizens United v. Federal Election Commission *ruling—a landmark US Supreme Court decision stating that corporate funding of independent political broadcasts in candidate elections cannot be limited—is overblown and that the greater risk to democracy is the denial of First Amendment rights. According to Schroder, the Bipartisan Campaign Reform Act of 2002 was inadequate to prevent the undue influ-*

Amy Schroder, "Citizens United: Electoral Apocalypse or Freedom?" *Nexus: Chapman's Journal of Law and Public Policy*, September 26, 2010. Copyright © 2010 by Nexus. Reproduced by permission.

ence of corporations, unions, and advocacy groups on elections, including the establishment of 527 organizations, through which corporate money can be funneled. Furthermore, says Schroder, the widespread reaction against the Citizens United *ruling presumes that individual voters are incapable of judging for themselves whether or not to support the issues and candidates that will appear in corporate-funded advertisements.*

As you read, consider the following questions:

1. According to the author, what did the 2002 Bipartisan Campaign Reform Act prohibit?

2. What are "527" organizations as described in the viewpoint?

3. Why does the author believe average people will still have the ability to influence elections despite the *Citizens United* ruling?

"America isn't easy. America is advanced citizenship. You gotta want it bad, 'cause it's gonna put up a fight. It's gonna say 'You want free speech?' Let's see you acknowledge a man whose words make your blood boil, who's standing center stage and advocating at the top of his lungs that which you would spend a lifetime opposing at the top of yours. You want to claim this land as the land of the free?" These are the words of the actor Michael Douglas playing the role of President of the United States in *The American President.* Now, while Hollywood often over-dramatizes real life, this scene focuses on a very salient point; free speech isn't just about my right to say what I want to say, it's about the right of everyone to say what they want to say. Many of us invoke the concept, the right, of free speech willy-nilly but do we really consider what that means?

Finance Legislation Was Already Weak

The United States Supreme Court in *Citizens United v. Federal Election Commission* addressed the issue of free speech as it pertains to certain corporate expenditures in the context of elections. The High Court held that a provision of the Bipartisan Campaign Reform Act prohibiting unions, corporations and not-for-profit organizations from broadcasting electioneering communications within 60 days of a general election or 30 days of a primary election violated the free speech clause of the First Amendment to the United States Constitution. The Bipartisan Campaign Reform Act of 2002 (BCRA) (aka McCain-Feingold), prohibited corporations and unions from using their general treasury funds to make an electioneering communication or for independent expenditures, defined as speech that expressly advocates the election or defeat of a candidate and that is made independently of a candidate's campaign. However, like almost every other piece of federal legislation, McCain-Feingold was full of holes, some of them large enough to drive a Mack Truck through. For example, under McCain-Feingold, corporations and unions were free to spend unlimited amounts of money on voter registration and get-out-the-vote activities directed at their stockholders, employees and members. Also within the purview of corporate "political" spending was setting up and running 527 organizations. Though 527 organizations cannot endorse a candidate, receive party funding, or collaborate with a candidate's campaign, there are no restrictions on opposing a candidate as long as the 527 organization is acting as a free agent. And while they might be funneling more money into campaigns through some of these independent groups, corporations had the right to make such contributions before the ruling. So, really and truly, the Court's decision in *Citizens United* did not doom the election landscape as much as some would make out.

Opponents of the *Citizens United* decision have made apocalyptic predictions that elections will now become bought and paid for by corporations and that those same corporations will control the single hair of a horse tail for incumbents sitting beneath Damocles sword. Opponents fear that the

The *Citizens United* Decision Upholds the First Amendment

Banning independent political advocacy violates the First Amendment because it effectively limits speech. The [US Supreme] Court rejected the idea that the government can decide who gets to speak and that the government can actually impose "federal felony punishment" on some for speaking at all, particularly those who speak through associations of members who share their beliefs.

The Court held that the First Amendment stands against attempts to distinguish among different speakers, which "are all too often simply a means to control content." In so doing, the Court correctly held that the government cannot impose restrictions on certain disfavored speakers such as corporations. The Court also found that First Amendment free speech rights do not depend on a speaker's financial ability to engage in public discussion: The fact that some speakers may have more wealth than others does not diminish their First Amendment rights.

Hans von Spakovsky,
"Citizens United and the Restoration of the First Amendment,"
The Heritage Foundation, February 17, 2010.

voice of the people will be drowned out by special interests and that the needs of individual Americans will play second fiddle to the desires of corporations. This concern is misplaced in that it presupposes that the American people are incapable of making their voices heard and that these same people are unable to avoid being persuaded by the onslaught of political ads we have all come to know and love. In this modern technological age, almost every voter has easy (if not instant) access to the Internet, with its blogs, social and business networking sites, and a myriad of other resources for registering complaints and advocating ideas. With this reality, is there really as strong an argument that the voices of the individual citizenry, the voices of the poor, tired and huddled masses will go unheard? Even President [Barack] Obama admitted, though I am certain it was unintentional, the unlikelihood that the *Citizens United* decision would defeat the will of "the People." In a recent radio address, the Commander in Chief encouraged the People that they "can make sure that the tens of millions of dollars spent on misleading ads do not drown out your voice, because no matter how many ads they run—no matter how many elections they try to buy—the power to determine the fate of this country doesn't lie in their hands. It lies in yours." That's right Mr. President. It is in our hands. It has always been in our hands and it will continue to be in our hands.

At the end of the day, the reality is that the money is coming in regardless of how much legislation is thrown at it. Therefore, the question then becomes whether or not we are willing to start denying fundamental rights in an effort to stop the cash. I say we err on the side of freedom and stop underestimating the ability of the People to sort through muck.

> *"The public backlash against the [Citizens United] decision . . . provided an opening for progressives to organize around a bold and far-reaching reform message."*

The *Citizens United* Decision Will Encourage Voters to Exercise Their First Amendment Rights

Ari Berman

Ari Berman is a contributing writer for the Nation. *In the following viewpoint, Berman foresees a much overdue populist uprising in response to the* Citizens United *ruling, which, according to him, will ultimately increase the ability of voters to exercise their First Amendment rights. For Berman, the Supreme Court's decision on* Citizens United *makes the threat of unlimited corporate influence in American elections more tangible to many voters, who may, according to Berman, use the ruling as an opportunity to organize formally around the effort to educate others and advocate for more reasonable campaign finance reform. Specifically, reformers plan to begin a multi-pronged effort to re-*

verse the Supreme Court's ruling through a Constitutional Amendment, advocating for the passage of the Fair Elections Now Act, and urging new legislation that will change the standards by which lobbyists operate.

As you read, consider the following questions:

1. According to Berman, what group is leading a "progressive response" to the *Citizens United* ruling?

2. What organization is notably exempt from the Democracy Is Strengthened by Casting Light on Spending in Elections (DISCLOSE) Act?

3. According to the author, by what means are New York City's public advocate and comptroller urging corporations to disclose their political donations?

A disturbing pattern has emerged repeatedly during [President] Barack Obama's turbulent tenure in Washington: no matter what piece of progressive-minded legislation gets introduced, powerful corporate interests find a way either to kill the bill or thwart the provisions our gilded class finds most onerous. Sometimes they succeed completely (the Employee Free Choice Act); other times they score partial victories (healthcare reform). But those with the most money rarely lose outright. And then came the Supreme Court's January 21 [2010] decision in *Citizens United v. Federal Election Commission*, which greenlights unlimited corporate spending in federal elections and grants corporations the same free-speech rights as individuals, severely impairing our already dilapidated democracy.

The Court's ruling prompted immediate despair among progressive activists. "This decision will warp our democracy forever if we let it do so," says New York City Public Advocate Bill de Blasio. No longer could the festering issue of corporate involvement in electoral and legislative politics be ignored or simply remain the province of "good government" activists.

Yet the public backlash against the decision—highlighted by President Obama's rare criticism of the Court during his first State of the Union address—provided an opening for progressives to organize around a bold and far-reaching reform message. "*Citizens United* was the breaking point for folks," says Ilyse Hogue, director of political advocacy and communications for MoveOn.org. "We needed a comprehensive vision, as a movement, for how to have a voice in our own democracy."

A Wide-Ranging Progressive Response

Starting in May [2010], MoveOn organized more than 150 community forums across the country and consulted with experts in the public policy, netroots and legal communities to craft a progressive response to *Citizens United*. In late June MoveOn members overwhelmingly approved a three-part "Fight Washington Corruption" pledge calling for (1) overturning the Court's decision through an amendment to the Constitution; (2) passing the Fair Elections Now Act in Congress, which incentivizes candidates to collect small donations by offering competitive public matching funds; and (3) enacting tough new laws cracking down on the revolving door between government officials and lobbyists. A diverse coalition of advocacy groups, including the SEIU [Service Employees International Union], Democracy for America (DFA), People for the American Way and *The Nation* signed on as co-sponsors. MoveOn called it "our most ambitious campaign ever."

The pledge has more than 400,000 signatures as of press time, and the goal is to gather 1 million by Election Day. Congressional candidates will be urged to sign it during the August recess, and by September, MoveOn plans to endorse those candidates who have enthusiastically embraced the reform message and target those who've most egregiously repudiated it—including corporate Democrats. "The goal is to make the election a referendum on corporate power," says Hogue. "For the first time, our members are sensing the need to go systemic." Frustrated by the lack of gains in the Obama era, MoveOn leader Sandra VanderVen, a real estate agent in Seattle [Washington], says members in her area are "excited to launch something huge and see where it goes."

There are no quick fixes to the Court's decision. "The fight for campaign finance reform and to overturn *Citizens United* is a multiyear, massive undertaking," says DFA political director Charles Chamberlain. An amendment to the Constitution hasn't passed in two decades. There is little appetite in Congress for stricter lobbying reforms. The Fair Elections Now Act, with 157 House co-sponsors, has the best chance of getting a vote and passing that body this year, but the math is much tougher in the Senate, where the bill has only twenty-two co-sponsors and has yet to receive a hearing in the Rules Committee. A legislative stopgap, the DISCLOSE [Democracy Is Strengthened by Casting Light on Spending in Elections] Act, which requires a wide array of political groups to list their donors and identify themselves in ads before the election, passed the House in June but doesn't yet have the sixty votes needed to break a Republican filibuster in the Senate. It also exempts a few lucky behemoths, most notably the NRA [National Rifle Association], from disclosure requirements, and, at best, offers a return to the broken, pre-*Citizens United* status quo. The bill's flaws only underscore the need for more fundamental and structural long-term reforms. "Progressives have to grapple with this central truth—we can't solve the country's problems if we don't fix the systems of democracy," says Michael Waldman, executive director of the Brennan Center for Justice at New York University. "This has been a missing argument for the first year and a half of the Obama administration."

The Impact of *Citizens United* Remains Unclear but Backlash Persists

There is still a debate in Washington [D.C.] over what kind of impact the Court's decision will have on future elections. Labor unions have thus far outspent corporations in post-*Citizens United* spending, but that imbalance will likely be reversed by November. Conservative groups, including the Chamber of Commerce and the [Republican political analyst] Karl Rove-backed American Crossroads, are already planning to spend $300 million in 2010 hammering Democratic candidates, according to a Democratic Party memo obtained by the *Washington Post*. "I'd be shocked if we went through this cycle without someone pulling the trigger," de Blasio says, noting that nothing—except the fear of a public backlash—prevents a company like ExxonMobil from unloading $1 million to influence a pivotal House or Senate race. De Blasio and New York City comptroller John Liu have been urging large financial firms like Bank of America to voluntarily disclose their political spending, with some success, by introducing shareholder resolutions and threatening consumer boycotts. "People have to feel like their spending could backfire tremendously," de Blasio says.

The aftershocks of *Citizens United* have initiated what Waldman calls "a mass teachable moment about the need for systemic reform." Combined with widespread public anger at big banks in the wake of the financial crisis, the time may be ripe for a Teddy Roosevelt-style populist crusade that transcends typical ideological barriers, linking the inequities in our economy to the staggering amount of money in our political system. "I don't really think this is just a progressive issue," says Keith Rouda, a MoveOn leader and business consultant in Louisville [Kentucky]. "Before we're done, it'll be a little odd and it'll feel a little weird, but I think we'll be marching down the street with some Tea Party people."

Periodical Bibliography

The following articles have been selected to supplement the diverse views presented in this chapter.

| Floyd Abrams and Burt Neuborne | "Debating 'Citizens United,'" *The Nation*, January 13, 2011. |

Stanley Fish — "What Is the First Amendment For?" *New York Times*, February 1, 2010.

Daniel J.H. Greenwood — "Money Is Speech: Why the *Citizens United v. FEC* Ruling Is Bad for Politics and the Market," *Dissent*, March 3, 2010.

Terence P. Jeffrey — "Chief Justice Roberts: Kagan Asked Court to 'Embrace Theory of First Amendment That Would Allow Censorship Not Only of Radio and Television Broadcasts, but Pamphlets and Posters,'" CNSnews.com, May 10, 2010.

David Kairys — "Money Isn't Speech and Corporations Aren't People," Slate.com, January 22, 2010.

Wendy Kaminer — "Citizens United, For and Against Free Speech," *The Atlantic*, February 5, 2010.

John Kramer — "Dispelling the Top Five *Citizens United* Decision Myths," Institute for Justice, January 26, 2010.

David Lat — "Why *Citizens United* Is Not the End of the World," AbovetheLaw.com, May 11, 2010.

Lawrence Lessig — "Democracy After *Citizens United*," *Boston Review*, September–October 2010.

Trevor Potter — "For a Small Amount of Doctrinal Gain, the *Citizens United* Majority Produced a Maximum Amount of Pain," *Campaign Legal Center Blog*, October 28, 2010.

For Further Discussion

Chapter 1

1. Paul Blumenthal advocates the use of real-time disclosure through online portals, saying it would increase transparency in political donations and encourage small donor activity. In January 2011, the Federal Election Commission rejected a proposal that would allow small donors to send donations via cell phone text messages. What are the pros and cons of using technology such as the Internet and cell phones for campaign donations in light of current campaign finance legislation?

2. John R. Lott Jr. and Bradley A. Smith advocate a completely anonymous system for campaign donation because they argue that mandatory disclosure can expose individuals to retaliation. Should personal safety be a concern when a person donates to a political campaign or referendum initiative? Why or why not?

3. Proponents and opponents of stricter disclosure laws argue that their positions will both lead to the same outcome: greater fiscal responsibility, more freedom of speech, and less political corruption. Which of their arguments do you find more compelling and why?

Chapter 2

1. Why does Daniel Weeks propose a new focus on small donors to counter the effects of big-money influence on elections? Do you think he is correct in believing that small donors would encourage accountability in the system?

2. David M. Primo claims to rely on "scientific research" to prove his points. Given the wide variety of positions on

publicly-funded elections in this chapter, do you think it is possible to use a scientific method to prove one's point on this subject?

Chapter 3

1. Chris Good's viewpoint features opinions from Trevor Potter and Scott Thomas, who are both former chairmen of the Federal Election Commission. Does this make you value their opinions on election financing more than the opinions of others? Why or why not? Should a person's background or experience always be taken into account when judging their opinions?

2. Hans A. von Spakovsky compares the DISCLOSE Act to the 1798 Alien and Sedition Acts that were passed by Congress during the administration of President John Adams in part to inhibit open criticism of the Federalist Party by newspapers and publishers. The Acts have since been declared largely unconstitutional. Does this seem to be a fair comparison to you? Why or why not?

3. Jesse Zwick considers the Federal Election Commission to be incapable of properly monitoring elections because of the partisanship that is built into its system. On the other hand, George F. Will believes the commission fulfills its purpose because, in his opinion, the campaign finance legislation that already exists is adequate and may even be overly regulatory. Which do you think is more important to monitor the campaign finance system: the commission charged with oversight or the legislation passed to regulate it? Or is the way they function equally important and interdependent?

4. Why are J. Gerald Hebert and Tara Malloy concerned about judicial cases that argue issues related to *Citizens United v. Federal Election Commission*? What effects will the Supreme Court's decisions on these cases have on future campaign finance reform? What do the rulings say about judicial neutrality?

Chapter 4

1. Floyd Abrams and Glenn Greenwald both contend that the First Amendment is the only basis on which the Supreme Court's *Citizens United v. Federal Election Commission* decision can be judged. Do you agree or disagree, and why? Is it fair to speculate on the possible future consequences of judicial rulings, or should they stand alone?

2. Supreet Minhas argues that corporations are inherently different than people, yet the US Supreme Court has a long history of granting constitutional rights to corporations and has distinguished between "natural persons" and "artificial persons" specifically for the purpose of establishing that corporations are to be granted a form of personhood. What do you think constitutes personhood? Should corporations and other organized groups of people be given the legal status of personhood even if they are not biologically persons?

3. Ian Millhiser expects the *Citizens United* ruling to result in a rise in corporate power within the political sphere and a drop in the power of ordinary voters. Ari Berman, on the other hand, foresees a popular uprising in reaction to the Supreme Court decision. Which prediction do you think is correct? Is there a finite amount of power in politics, or can individuals and small groups compete against corporations in influencing elections?

Organizations to Contact

The editors have compiled the following list of organizations concerned with the issues debated in this book. The descriptions are derived from materials provided by the organizations. All have publications or information available for interested readers. The list was compiled on the date of publication of the present volume; names, addresses, phone and fax numbers, and e-mail and Internet addresses may change. Be aware that many organizations take several weeks or longer to respond to inquiries, so allow as much time as possible.

American Civil Liberties Union (ACLU)
125 Broad St., 18th Floor, New York, NY   10004
(212) 549-2500
website: www.aclu.org

The American Civil Liberties Union is a legal, advocacy, and watchdog group dedicated to ensuring that First Amendment, due process, equal protection, and privacy laws are upheld. In this role, the ACLU opposes campaign spending and disclosure laws that the group believes violate individual rights to free speech and privacy.

Brennan Center for Justice at New York University School of Law
161 Avenue of the Americas, 12th Floor, New York, NY   10013
(212) 998-6730 • fax: (212) 995-4550
e-mail: brennancenter@nyu.edu
website: www.brennancenter.org

The Brennan Center for Justice at New York University School of Law is a research, education, and advocacy organization that focuses on concerns related to democracy and justice. In June 2009, the center hosted the conference, "Money in Politics 2009: New Horizons for Reform," publications from which are available on its website. The center's website also publishes articles, reports, and commentary, including *Electoral Competition and Low Contribution Limits* and *Breaking Free with Fair Elections.*

Campaign Finance Institute (CFI)

1667 K St. NW, Suite 650, Washington, DC   20006
(202) 969-8890 • fax: (202) 969-5612
e-mail: info@cfinst.org
website: www.cfinst.org

The Campaign Finance Institute is a nonprofit and nonpartisan research organization that studies issues related to campaign finance and develops reports and recommendations for government officials and the general public. CFI tracks political party fundraising and contributions to and spending by congressional and presidential candidates. Many of CFI's publications are available on the institute's website.

Campaign Legal Center (CLC)

215 E St. NE, Washington, DC   20002
(202) 736-2200 • fax: (202) 736-2222
e-mail: info@campaignlegalcenter.org
website: www.campaignlegalcenter.org.

The Campaign Legal Center is a research and public advocacy organization that examines the legal issues surrounding campaign finance and election law. The center tracks legal cases and issues reports and comments to the Federal Election Commission. Its Media Policy Program lobbies on behalf of open broadcast airwaves and participates in public forums on campaign media legislation. On its website, CLC publishes fact sheets, weekly reports, and articles of interest on current cases, Federal Election Commission proceedings, campaign finance reform, and redistricting.

Cato Institute

1000 Massachusetts Ave. NW, Washington, DC   20001-5403
(202) 842-0200 • fax: (202) 842-3490
website: www.cato.org

The Cato Institute is a conservative think tank, founded in 1977, that performs public policy research and publishes papers about small government, free markets, and individual liberty. Among other interests, the organization advocates for limited government interference in the election process, including opposing stricter disclosure legislation and supporting First Amendment issues concerning campaign spending.

Center for American Progress Action Fund
1333 H St. NW, 10th Floor, Washington, DC   20005
(202) 682-1611 • fax: (202) 682-1867
website: www.americanprogress.org

The Center for American Progress Action Fund is an organization that advocates for the enactment of progressive policies. The group's focus is on domestic, economic, and national security issues, and its blog, ThinkProgress.org, often addresses matters related to the elections system.

Center for Competitive Politics (CCP)
901 N Glebe Rd., Suite 900, Arlington, VA   22203
(703) 682-9359 • fax: (703) 682-9321
e-mail: info@campaignfreedom.org
website: www.campaignfreedom.org.

The Center for Competitive Politics was founded in 2005 by former Federal Election Commission Chairman Bradley A. Smith. It promotes a more fair and open electoral process. The center publishes legal briefs, reports, and studies on campaign finance, many of which are available on its website. Center members often testify before Congress and other public bodies, and testimony transcripts also are available online.

Center for Public Integrity
910 17th St. NW, Suite 700, Washington, DC   20006
(202) 466-1300
website: www.publicintegrity.org

The Center for Public Integrity is a nonprofit organization dedicated to supporting, producing, and disseminating investigative journalism, particularly in the interest of increasing government transparency. The group generates reports and maintains databases on its website, including those related to campaign spending.

Center for Responsive Politics (CRP)

1101 14th St. NW, Suite 1030, Washington, DC   20005-5635
(202) 857-0044 • fax: (202) 857-7809
e-mail: info@crp.org
website: www.opensecrets.org

The Center for Responsive Politics tracks money in politics and its effect on public policy. Its website, OpenSecrets.org, provides detailed information on funding sources for presidential and congressional incumbents and challengers as well as political action committees (PACs) and 527 organizations. The center publishes the newsletter *Capital Eye* and numerous reports, including *The Millionaire on the Ballot* and *Shopping in (Partisan) Style*, which are available on its website.

Common Cause

1133 19th St. NW, 9th Floor, Washington, DC   20036
(202) 833-1200
e-mail: grassroots@commoncause.org
website: www.commoncause.org

Founded in 1970, Common Cause is a nonprofit, nonpartisan, advocacy group. Its goal is to hold elected leaders accountable to the American people. Common Cause promotes a variety of activist causes such as campaign finance reform, voter registration drives, and openness in government. It has led voter mobilization drives prior to presidential elections and efforts to enact public financing of elections at the state level. Its website has an archive of its online journal, *Common Cause Magazine*, and links to other publications, including research papers, press releases, and blogs.

Democracy 21

2000 Massachusetts Ave. NW, Washington, DC   20036
(202) 355-9600 • fax: (202) 355-9606

e-mail: info@democracy21.org
website: www.democracy21.org

Founded in 1997 by former Common Cause president Fred Wertheimer, Democracy 21 works to eliminate the undue influence of big money in American politics and to ensure the integrity and fairness of government decisions and elections. The organization promotes campaign finance reform and other political reforms to accomplish these goals. Democracy 21 publishes issue papers about the Bipartisan Campaign Reform Act, public financing, the Federal Election Commission, and 527 organizations.

Federal Election Commission (FEC)

999 E St. NW, Washington, DC   20463
(800) 424-9530
e-mail: info@fec.gov
website: www.fec.gov

Created by Congress as an independent regulatory agency in 1975, the Federal Election Commission administers and enforces the Federal Election Campaign Act, the legislation that governs the financing of federal elections. The FEC discloses campaign finance information, enforces the provisions of the law such as the limits and prohibitions on contributions, and oversees the public funding of presidential elections.

Institute for Justice (IJ)

901 N Glebe Rd., Suite 900, Arlington, VA   22203
(703) 682-9320 • fax: (703) 682-9321
e-mail: general@ij.org
website: www.ij.org

Founded in 1991, the Institute for Justice is the only law firm in the United States that exclusively handles cases in which civil liberties are being challenged. Supporters of the Supreme Court's 2010 decision in *Citizens United v. Federal Election Commission*, IJ publishes a blog, Congress Shall Make No Law, on which it comments on issues related to free speech and privacy rights.

Progressive Policy Institute (PPI)

1730 Rhode Island Ave. NW, Suite 308
Washington, DC 20036
(202) 525-3926 • fax: (202) 525-3941
e-mail: ppi_admin@ppionline.org
website: www.ppionline.org

The Progressive Policy Institute is a research and education program of the Third Way Foundation, Inc., whose goal is to advance a political philosophy that is neither liberal nor conservative but rather one in keeping with the realities of life in the twenty-first century age of information. PPI lists one of its main strategies as advancing democracy by giving citizens greater control of the political process, including the way political campaigns are organized and funded.

Public Campaign

1320 19th St. NW, Suite M-1, Washington, DC 20036
(202) 293-0222 • fax: (202) 293-0202
e-mail: mengle@publiccampaign.org
website: www.publiccampaign.org

Public Campaign is a nonpartisan campaign finance reform organization that seeks to reduce the role of special interest money in American politics. It publishes educational materials on various campaign reform measures and provides news, polling data, and commentary on money in politics on its website.

Sunlight Foundation

1818 N St. NW, Suite 300, Washington, DC 20036
(202) 742-1520
website: www.sunlightfoundation.com

The Sunlight Foundation is a nonprofit and nonpartisan organization that seeks to gain greater government transparency through the use of modern technology. With a board and advisory group made up of the heads of major American corporations, the Sunlight Foundation offers grants to organizations that use the Internet to provide Americans with greater access to the workings of their government, including the way its political campaigns are funded.

Bibliography of Books

Floyd Abrams · *Speaking Freely: Trials of the First Amendment*. New York: Penguin, 2005.

Bruce Ackerman and Ian Ayres · *Voting with Dollars: A New Paradigm for Campaign Finance*. New Haven, CT: Yale University Press, 2004.

Janet M. Box-Steffensmeier · *The Elections of 2008*. Lanham, MD: Rowman and Littlefield, 2009.

California Voter Foundation · *Grading State Disclosure, 2008: Evaluating States' Efforts to Bring Sunlight to Political Money*. Sacramento, CA: Campaign Disclosure Project, 2008.

Erwin Chemerinsky · *The Conservative Assault on the Constitution*. New York: Simon and Schuster, 2010.

Marian Currinder · *Money in the House: Campaign Funds and Congressional Party Politics*. Boulder, CO: Westview Press, 2008.

Victoria A. Farrar-Myers and Diana Dwyre · *Limits and Loopholes: The Quest for Money, Free Speech, and Fair Elections*. Washington, DC: CQ Press, 2007.

Peter L. Francia, John C. Green, Paul S. Herrnson, Lynda W. Powell, and Clyde Wilcox · *The Financiers of Congressional Elections: Investors, Ideologues, and Intimates*. New York: Columbia University Press, 2003.

Michael M. Franz   *Choices and Changes: Interest Groups in the Electoral Process.* Philadelphia, PA: Temple University Press, 2008.

R. Sam Garrett   *Public Financing of Congressional Elections.* Hauppauge, NY: Nova Science Publishers, 2008.

Henry A. Giroux   *Zombie Politics and Culture in the Age of Casino Capitalism.* New York: Peter Lang, 2010.

J. Tobin Grant and Thomas J. Rudolph   *Expression vs. Equality: Politics of Campaign Finance Reform.* Columbus, OH: Ohio State University Press, 2004.

Mark J. Green   *Selling Out: How Big Corporate Money Buys Elections, Rams Through Legislation, and Betrays Our Democracy.* New York: Harper, 2004.

Thom Hartmann   *Unequal Protection: How Corporations Became "People"—and How You Can Fight Back.* San Francisco, CA: Berrett-Koehler, 2010.

Paul S. Herrnson   *Congressional Elections: Campaigning at Home and in Washington.* Washington, DC: CQ Press, 2007.

Robert G. Kaiser   *So Damn Much Money: The Triumph of Lobbying and the Corrosion of American Government.* New York: Vintage, 2010.

Ray LaRaja — *Small Change: Money, Political Parties, and Campaign Finance Reform*. Ann Arbor, MI: University of Michigan Press, 2008.

David B. Magleby, Anthony Corrado, and Kelly D. Patterson — *Financing the 2004 Election*. Washington, DC: Brookings Institution Press, 2006.

Alan L. Moss — *Selling Out America's Democracy: How Lobbyists, Special Interests, and Campaign Financing Undermine the Will of the People*. New York: Praeger, 2008.

John Samples — *Welfare for Politicians? Taxpayer Financing of Political Campaigns*. Washington, DC: Cato Institute, 2005.

John Samples — *The Fallacy of Campaign Finance Reform*. Chicago, IL: University of Chicago Press, 2006.

Frederic Charles Schaffer — *The Hidden Costs of Clean Election Reform*. New York: Cornell University Press, 2008.

Bradley A. Smith — *Unfree Speech: The Folly of Campaign Finance Reform*. Princeton, NJ: Princeton University Press, 2003.

Melissa Smith — *Campaign Finance Reform: The Political Shell Game*. Lanham, MD: Lexington Books, 2010.

Rodney A. Smith   *Money, Power, and Elections: How Campaign Finance Reform Subverts American Democracy.* Baton Rouge, LA: Louisiana State University Press, 2006.

Matthew J. Streb   *Rethinking American Electoral Democracy.* New York: Routledge, 2008.

Supreme Court of   *So Much for Democracy:* Citizens
the United States   United v. Federal Election Commission. Ann Arbor, MI: Nimble Books, 2009.

Melvin I. Urofsky   *Money and Free Speech: Campaign Finance and the Courts.* Lawrence, KS: University of Kansas Press, 2005.

Peter J. Wallison   *Better Parties, Better Government: A*
and Joel M. Gora   *Realistic Program for Campaign Finance Reform.* Washington, DC: AEI Press, 2009.

Darrell M. West   *Air Wars: Television Advertising in Election Campaigns, 1952–2008.* Washington, DC: CQ Press, 2009.

Index